Trees of Sheepscombe

An exploration and appreciation of more than fifty trees to be found in the woods, commons and gardens of this Cotswold village. Including natives, newcomers, exotics and some dinosaurs.

Peter Collings-Wells

White Spring Books

Opposite: The path up to the woods and the common from Far End Lane.
Content pages: The valley edge of Workmans Wood in winter.

To the Woods!

Contents / Index

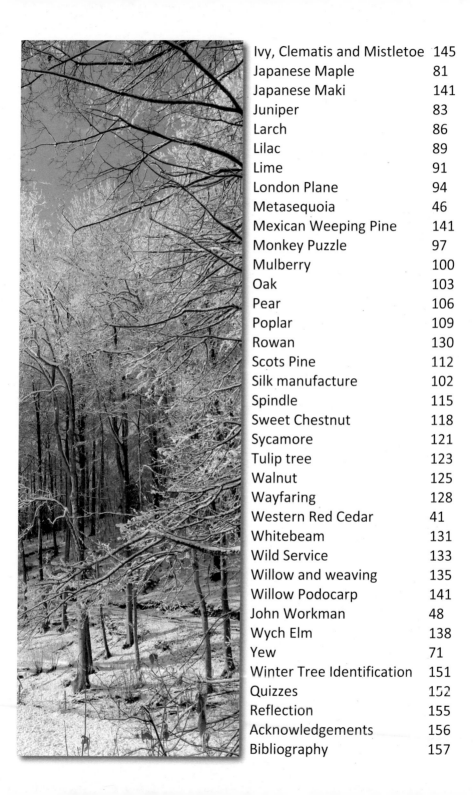

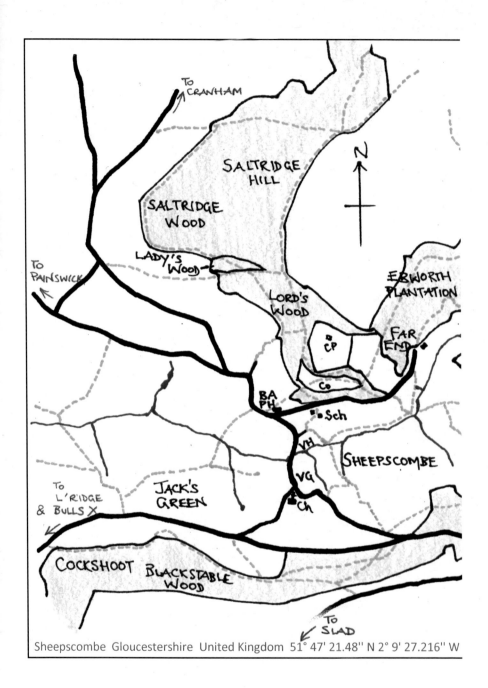

Sheepscombe Gloucestershire United Kingdom 51° 47' 21.48'' N 2° 9' 27.216'' W

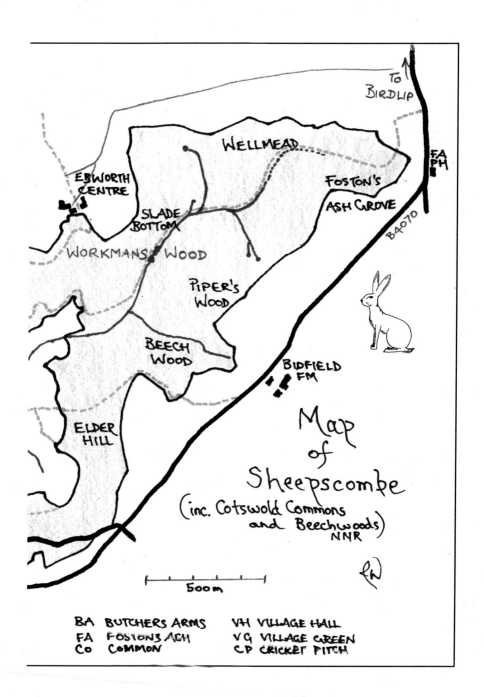

Map
of
Sheepscombe
(inc. Cotswold Commons
and Beechwoods)
NNR

500m

BA BUTCHERS ARMS   VH VILLAGE HALL
FA FOSTONS ASH   VG VILLAGE GREEN
Co COMMON   CP CRICKET PITCH

7

Introduction

Let's go for a walk. Any one of the dozen or more that strike upwards from the village will do. There's quite a lot of up, but it's worth it. Very quickly we'll find ourselves passing through the hazel belt, once diligently coppiced for charcoal and poles. If we're quiet we might spot a deer or two, alert and watchful in the dappled afternoon sun. Climbing on up we find ourselves on a Common dotted with birch, whitebeam, gorse and oak and being watched by gentle belted Galloway cattle. In the summer there is a carpet of wild-flowers, herbs and orchids here.

After a pause on the bench that looks out over the valley, we might continue on through the gate and into the woods. Here we pass into another world entirely. Massive beech trunks soar up all around and there's the air of having walked into a cathedral. Holly and yew are happy to live under this rather dominating canopy. There is ash, oak, wych elm and larch here, competing for light, but they are few and far between.

But wait. Let's stop awhile. Some of these trees are several of our lifetimes old, and surely they follow a slower clock. I find I need to be with a tree or in my favourite sit-spot at least half an hour to begin to tune in. Or if it's sunny, I let the hour hand of the tree's shadow be my guide.

There's something else too. Tiny sounds down in the forest floor. When beechnuts are in season you may hear the tiny plop of the husks hitting the ground, discarded by squirrels high above. And if you're by the foot of a Scots pine or larch and tune in, you may be able to pick out the whisper of a thousand wood ants going about their business on their pine-needle home.

Soon the path climbs again and after a while the gradient eases a little. We are almost at the top now and on the edge of a mixed plantation of Scots pine and larch. Up on the level, we are into the bright and broad world of the Cotswold plateau. You may hear the 'cronk' of raven flying high overhead. Several paths lead off and our journey continues . . .

So gentle reader, whichever path you're on, I hope that this book inspires you to enjoy, protect and connect with the glorious woodlands that surround and support us.

The Woods

Clothing the shoulders of the Sheepscombe and Cranham valleys, is an extensive collection of beautiful inter-linked woodlands and limestone grasslands. Much of the area is designated as the Cotswold Commons and Beechwoods National Nature Reserve (NNR). Around Sheepscombe this is made up of: Workmans Wood, Saltridge Wood, Lord's and Lady's Woods and Blackstable Wood - managed jointly by the National Trust and Natural England. Sheepscombe Common, St George's Field and Bulls Cross Common are managed by Natural England. Here you can walk for hours with only an occasional road (see map on pages 6&7).

Workmans Wood fills the upper end of the Sheepscombe valley and is by far the biggest woodland area (about 300 acres). It is formed of seven separate smaller woods - Beech Wood, Pipers Wood, Wellmead, Fostons Ash Grove, Butlers Grove and the Ebworth plantation. It is an SSSI[1] and in 1976 was declared an NNR and named 'Workmans Wood' by John Workman.[2] This was the year that his father Ernest would have been one hundred.

The land had been part of the ancient estate of Ebworth since 1066, and having had multiple owners since then, was bought by Henry Workman in 1901. They owned a sawmill and a timber merchant business at Woodchester near Stroud for much for the 18th century and the purchase of the woodland was largely in order to guarantee supplies.

The various logging tracks throughout the woods were designed so that the majority of the timber was within reach of a 50m hauling line. At that time there was a strong market for furniture, staircases and other objects made from beech. In 1989 John Workman gave the estate to the National Trust.

The wood is predominantly a beech plantation, with some ash, larch, Scots pine, a sprinkling of wych elm and an under-story of yew, holly hazel and some box. Among the trees you can find plants such stinking hellebore, common wintergreen, bird's-nest orchid, wood barley and broad-leaved helleborine. There are many charcoal platforms within the woods, which were active in the C18 and C19th.

There are four rights of way winding through the wood, the longest of which starts at Far End and follows the valley right up to the road near the Foston's Ash pub.

Sheepscombe from the air, winter 2019. Looking east-south-east. The valley runs in from west to east, before turning north-east and narrowing. From left: Lady's and Lord's, Workmans and Blackstable Woods.   Photo by Roger Banks

Saltridge Hill and Wood. These woods lie between Sheepscombe and Cranham, and sit high on a wide nose of the Cotswold escarpment overlooking the confluence of the Sheepscombe and Cranham valleys.

On its sloping western flanks, **Saltridge Wood** is mainly beech, together with wych elm, oak and ash. Above on the brow, **Saltridge Hill** is a plantation of mainly larch and Scots pine, planted around 1948 and covers around 75 acres. The logging road network here is laid out in the shape of the Union Flag. As elsewhere the plantation is dotted with conifers in order to 'nurse' the beech (encourage it to grow tall and straight). The felling cycle for conifers and beech was 50 and 100 years respectively. There are two rights of way, one along the eastern flank - part of an ancient route from Sheepscombe (possibly an old salt route), which then swings north-east towards Birdlip. The other is around the western edge of the wood.

Lord's and Lady's Woods are just to the north of the village, on the southern slopes of Saltridge Hill. They lie on either side of what was an entrance drive to the original Ebworth Estate, coming in from the road at Trench Hill. Lord's is much the larger, to the south of the track and around to the cricket pitch, with Lady's a small wedge just to the north. It is unclear where the names originated, but one theory is that the woods were originally owned by the Lords of the Manor. Both are predominantly planted beech interspersed with occasional larch and Scots pine and with some self-sown ash. These woods are Access Land, so you are free to roam anywhere within the boundaries. (See page 134 for explanation of the coloured markings on some of the trees)

Lord's Wood affords some magnificent views south-west down the valley to Painswick and beyond, especially magical in the evenings. There is a dense enclave of yew and holly above Magpie Bottom. In the summer months, bats hunt along the wood-edge, expertly dodging trees and visitors.

Blackstable Wood lies along the ridge to the south of the village in a long thin strip to the west, rounds a corner at Cockshoot and extends a little way along Longridge, about 65 acres in all. Up until around 1820 this was known as Longridge Wood. This is another predominantly beech plantation. The land was bought by the Workman family in the late 1800s again as a source of timber for their mills. Within the wood there is a 'Champion' beech, possibly the tallest in the country. This is Access Land, so you can walk anywhere within the boundary.

[1] SSSI Site of Special Scientific Interest   [2] See page 48 for more on John Workman

The Village Hall **alder** in winter, and its trunk.

The ancient black alder down by the stream below Painswick Lodge, just off the valley footpath. Although largely hollow now, it is still putting out good leaf.

Alder
(Alnus glutinosa)

Next time you're in the village hall car park, take a look at the rather magnificent six-trunked alder, standing guard. It's no accident that it has grown there - they love water and you'll see quite a number of others all along the Sheepscombe stream.

Alder is part of the birch family and is also a pioneer species, meaning that it is one of the first and quickest to grow in a cleared area.

Stand-out characteristics are largely horizontal branches, and the presence of both male catkins and female cones (also called catkins) on the same tree. The deciduous leaves tend to be oval, toothed, but with a flattened end, often with an indentation.

The bark is brown/grey and fissured with young twigs and root nodules having an orange colour. The leaves, twigs and bark are unpalatable to animals and thus aren't high on the list for rabbit and deer snacking.

The male catkins are yellow in spring and hang down tail-like, while the cones hang in groups, green and oval. The flowers appear around March before the leaves. In autumn, cones release little flat, red-brown seeds each encased in a small air-filled membrane that disperse in the wind and will float on water.

Alder can grow up to 20-25m tall and doesn't produce seeds until it is at least 20 years old. The empty cones often stay on the tree into winter and are helpful in identification.

Given its affinity with water it is probably not surprising that alder wood is prized for its durability when wet, and was widely used in boat-building, piling and in lock gates. Much of Venice is built on alder piling.

In folklore, some negative superstitions grew up around the fact that when cut, alder exhibits a rich orange colour akin to a wound and some would say it was unlucky to pass by one on your journey and worse to chop one down. But perhaps by the same token, in Celtic legend its properties were allied to that of a warrior or fighter, especially for its strength in water.

Possibly spread to Northern Ireland from Southern Europe after the last Ice Age around 7,000 years ago, the alder is known as *Fearnog* in Gaelic, hence Glenfarne in Co Leitrim, which means 'Valley of alders' and in the UK we have Northallerton in Yorkshire - 'North alder town'.

Cones and catkins

On a different note, and for all you rock 'n rollers out there, Fender have been making their famous electric guitars from alder since the 1950's as they found it sounds better than the ash they used to use.

Alder does not make the best firewood for although it will give off good heat, its low density means it burns rather fast.

Historically, alder would have been coppiced and made into charcoal which was much in demand in the making of gunpowder, when

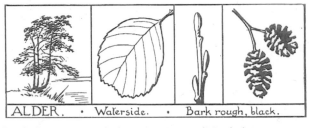

ALDER. • Waterside. • Bark rough, black.

the latter was popular for fighting wars and instigating political change.

It's well worth the walk down to find the ancient black alder by the valley footpath near the confluence of the Cranham and Sheepscombe streams. It is believed to be one of the oldest in the UK and was estimated to be 450 back in 1973 making it 500 years old now. In 2018 its girth was measured at 6m.

Alder also has the unusual property of being able to fix atmospheric nitrogen into the soil, thus allowing barren land to support more plant life.

A very beneficial pioneer indeed.

Ash

(Fraxinus excelsior)

Often to be seen punctuating our hedgerows or at field corners, ash is one of our most recognisable trees, summer or winter. It is a tough, deciduous species with straight-grained, springy wood, and in our valley can rise tall and slender to grab its patch of sky amongst competing beeches.

Ash leaves are compound with five to eleven pairs of leaflets growing opposite each other with one at the tip. Ash loves water, and one of its clever tricks is that each leaflet has a small groove running down the middle, almost covered in tiny hairs, and these channel and absorb rain. Leaves are relatively short-lived on the tree, being one of the last to leaf and first to drop in autumn - falling green. In these days of weather extremes I'm not sure how true is the old adage: "If the ash leafs before the oak, we are in for a soak, but if the oak leafs before the ash we are in for merely a splash."

For the budding student of tree recognition, ash is a great place to start. Its graceful branches sweep down and then curve up at the end, with the tell-tale sooty leaf buds at the tip.

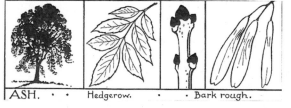

ASH. · ·   Hedgerow.   ·   · Bark rough.

Ash twigs are slightly flattened, and the "keys" - likened to gaolers keys - are the seed wings, and will often stay drooping from branches well into winter. These are shaped to spin down to the ground - hopefully catching wind and distance - like sycamore and field maple seeds.

The ash flowers in spring before it leafs, and is remarkable in producing purple-headed stamens that are without petals or sepals. Usually each flower has male and female parts but occasionally one or other part fails and the tree develops without seeds - keep an eye out for ash without keys after the summer.

Ash bark is smooth and grey when young, developing upright ridges with age, that can look like wave-edges on the beach. It is a dense wood that burns well in our hearths and log-burners, only surpassed by oak.

In folk-law, the ash was thought to have medicinal and mystical properties and the wood burned to ward off evil spirits. A sacred tree for Druids, its branches make good wands due to the straight and flexible grain.

In Norse mythology, it was referred to as the 'Tree of Life'. Both the Vikings and Gaels thought of ash as protective, and it is said that of the five legendary guardian trees of Ireland, three were ash. It is often found growing beside

Irish holy wells, and on the Isle of Man it was thought to protect the purity of springs.

Ash provides an excellent habitat for a number of different species of wildlife. The airy canopy and early leaf-fall allow sunlight to reach the woodland floor, so wildflowers such as dog violet, wild garlic and dogs mercury will grow underneath. Bullfinches eat the seeds and woodpeckers, owls, redstarts and nuthatches use the trees for nesting. Hazel grows well under ash, enjoying the light.

Humans too appreciate the strengths and flexibility of ash wood for furniture, implements, tools and for early carriage axles.

The Morris Traveller, that quintessential symbol of British country motoring, used to have a wooden ash frame, and I have heard of one example enduring many years on the rough and rutted roads of Africa, where man-made steel-framed vehicles would have cracked their welds or buckled under the strain. Clearly it pays to be flexible.

Ash on the green - note: almost no keys, and a number of dead branches due to "die-back" Inset: bare twig, autumn keys and leaf. Sadly it has had to be felled.

The magical six-trunked **ash** in Workmans Wood, up by the Spirit of the Woods carving. This has probably grown from an original coppicing around 50 years ago.

Aspen

(Populus tremula)

Despite being only partly-clad when I visited in mid-November, this character was rustling away loudly to the nearby sheep even though there wasn't a breath of wind in the valley.

Although this is a solo specimen, aspen can reproduce vegetatively or asexually by means of suckers or ramets. These are shoots produced by old roots, and may appear many metres away from the parent tree. All the trees in a given area may be connected through their root system and are therefore clones and will come into flower and leaf at the same time.

Pollination plays its part too of course, and aspen produces either male or female fluffy catkins in March or April. As the female catkins disperse on the wind, large quantities can cover the ground like fluffy spring snow.

Aspens prefer light to shade and and are often found in well-drained soil near rivers. Deer and cattle are fond of the leaves and this example is growing in the field across the brook from Coldstream Cottages, with a small protective fence all round. If you look from the field gate you will also spot a rare spindle tree to the left.

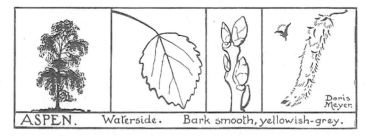

ASPEN.   Waterside.   Bark smooth, yellowish-grey.

Part of the poplar family, aspen is deciduous and characterised by slim, sparse upwards-growing branches with rounded crinkle-edged leaves.

The stems are flattened at right angles to the leaf blade and this is what allows them to tremble and wave when all else is still. As well as the delightful rustling this gives the visual effect of shimmering from a distance.

The **aspen** in the field opposite Coldstream
Cottages, in early winter. Spot the spindle.

Aspen can grow to 10 - 12 metres with a broad crown, but it is their cousin the Lombardy or black poplar that are tall and slim and often found in avenues.

This is another pioneer species, along with birch and alder, one of the first trees to colonise an area of waste ground that has either been cleared by human activity or by fire.

The wood is lightweight and straight-grained but rather prone to splitting. It's commonly used for matches where its low flammability makes it more suitable than other wood.

For identification in winter you really only have the tree shape, that its twigs are very knobbly, and the bark which is grey, generally smooth but broken up by diamond-shaped pores or 'lenticles'.

Catkins   (Sergei Sazhin - Wiki)

To mythology and symbolism, it is said that a crown of aspen leaves could give its wearer the power to visit and return safely from the Underworld. Aspen crowns found in ancient burial mounds may have been included to allow the spirits of the deceased to be reborn. Christian legend speaks of aspen quavering with remorse for being the wood that the Cross was made from.

In Celtic mythology, the sight and sound of aspen leaves trembling was thought to indicate that the tree was communicating with the gods.

And you know, in the few minutes I spent in the company of this one, its reassuring rustling took me to an altogether different plane.

(This tree is on private land - but it is visible from the road)

The majestic **beech** tunnel down from the Birdlip road.

Beech

(Fagus sylvatica)

Lofty and majestic, the beeches of Sheepscombe clothe most of the upper slopes of our valley. They are quite densely packed in places, and compete so vigorously with each other for light, that many have grown ram-rod straight some 30m tall or more. Such is their determination to own their own piece of sky, they show little or no side branch development until much higher up.

Stepping through the gate into the Ebworth plantations from St George's Field is always striking and uplifting, however many times I walk there. Beech leaves

take a long time to decay and there is always a crispy carpet of last year's fallen leaves to crunch through. On evening walks, often the only reason we notice deer or badger as they go about their business is the tell-tale rustling.

All is not sweetness and light in the beech world however. Along with the thick carpet of

Beech trunk and last year's leaves

leaf-litter, beech stays in leaf for a long season with a very dense canopy.

Together this means that very little light reaches down to the forest floor, and undergrowth finds it hard to get established, save for the occasional yew or holly. Without light, warmth and tempting flowers, flying bugs and bees don't venture in and so neither do birds. Where these woods are managed, clearings and rides are incorporated to allow light and breeze to enter and for more diversity to flourish.

For all beech's apparent strength and splendour, it hides a couple of weaknesses - the roots tend to be quite shallow - especially in our stony soil - and high winds can easily topple an exposed tree. They are also prey to the tinder bracket fungus which can attack the roots, trunk or branches invisibly from the inside. The only clue to this invasion is the sudden falling of an apparently healthy branch.

It's best not to camp or have an extended picnic in a beech wood, especially if it's windy.

Before the leaf canopy gets too full, bluebells and wild garlic take advantage of the available light to give us the delightful carpets of blue and white and green (and the aromas) that we enjoy so much.

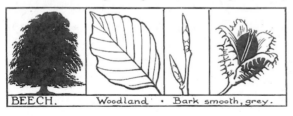
BEECH.   Woodland   •   Bark smooth, grey.

Beech bark is usually smooth, silver-grey and quite fragile. The cambium layer (where all the new growth happens) is very near the surface and thus susceptible to damage. The leaf-buds in winter are long, pointed and chestnut brown, and by April these have enlarged and open to reveal the soft, vibrant green leaves, which by summer have hardened and darkened.

With autumn frosts these turn yellow and gold and give us another splendid display of colour. By contrast, copper beech is a cultivated variant - there are one or two in the village - and have leaves of a red or purple hue and with a wavy/hairy edge as opposed to the serrated edge of the common beech.

The male catkins hang like green tassels on long stalks, and female flowers (surrounded by a cup) appear in April and May. This cup becomes woody once pollinated and grows within it one or two beechnuts - known as beechmast. The nuts can be food for jays, brambling, wood mice or fed to pigs.

Beech is a fine-grained hardwood, good for furniture or kitchen implement making as it is quite pliable when steamed and easily carved, however it is not favoured for use outdoors as it rots easily. It does make good firewood, but takes longer than some to dry out due to its high initial water content.

It is associated with wisdom and knowledge, with beech as the Queen of the woodland where oak is the King. There is a disputed theory that beech wood was amongst the first surfaces that humans wrote on, possibly in runic writing. In Swedish the word for 'beech' is *bok* which also means book, and the Anglo-Saxon is also *bok* which developed into 'book'.

Helen of Troy is said to have carved her and her lover's name on a beech tree - along with countless others since. Tut-tut!

Fern-leaf beech (Fagus sylvatica 'asplenifolia')
Copper (Purpurea), *Weeping* (Pendula)

Our classic beech is so distinctive and prevalent around here that I thought I could identify one at a hundred paces. Consequently I was flummoxed a while ago to find myself in the dappled shade of a tree that was at once beech and yet not beech. Schrödinger's tree perhaps?

Ok, back to basics - smooth grey-green bark with some mottled markings, alternate buds and leaves growing close to the twig, which themselves fan out sweeping from the branch - all beech identifiers.

But the leaves? Artistically serrated as if lifted from a Tolkien drawing, they give this specimen an altogether more elegant and fairy-tale feel and are not beech-shaped at all! Fascinated and perplexed, I took lots of photos, and went home to research.

Also known as cut-leaf beech, these were introduced to the UK in the 1800s, and are a cultivar of the common beech *(fagus sylvatica)*, selected for their ornamental beauty. This one is showing the typical pyramidal shape and the fern-like leaves are due to turn a striking yellow soon.

> Cultivar or variety? A cultivar is a plant or tree that has been produced through grafting or a cutting, doesn't occur naturally in the wild, and won't grow from seed. A variety is one that develops naturally from cross-pollination and is then chosen for commercial propagation to maintain its desired characteristics.

Other beech cultivars include copper (*purpurea*) - there's a huge one in the grounds of The Old Vicarage , weeping (*pendula*) - by the edge of the cricket pitch, and there's also dwarf (*tortuosa*) - with twisted trunk and branches.

Interestingly, if the tree is damaged and new leaves grow, they will often be those of the common beech, the core stock. This is the case here if you look at its eastern (up-valley) side. So is that nature or nurture?

This is one delightful if confused tree.

The shapely **fern-leaf beech** in the field below the Far End post box. But can you find the branch bearing original stock leaves?

Two other cultivars of **beech**: copper and weeping.
The Old Vicarage and the cricket pitch.

The fallen giant

1860s-2022

Late October and early November 2022

(Upper photo: Frances Day)

The John Workman Tree

By Tom Griffin - National Trust Area Ranger

The tree was given this name because it was one of John's favourites on the estate. It was an old pollard, grown when the land around it was open. This is shown by the many shoots coming from the trunk and its wide spreading nature. The trees now growing around it were planted when the tree was already well mature.

Frances Day

The fungus Ganoderma was well established on the tree. This species breaks down the lignin in the wood causing rot. It was this rot around the base of the tree which effectively severed the bulk of the tree from its roots allowing it to blow over.

We had been keeping a close eye on the fungi infecting the tree and monitored the health of the crown. As sometimes happens the extent of the rot inside the tree was not visible externally. It falling did come as a bit of a surprise.

Beech are particularly susceptible to drought because of their shallow roots. This makes them a species of concern with the effects of climate change. The very hot, dry summer of 2022 has had an effect on the growth of the tree but it was the rot which ultimately killed it.

We have now made the beech safe. Leaving the trunk in situ as a monument. Its seeds have been collected and will be grown on to be planted out in the same location as a replacement to this really special tree.

A ring was cut from the base of one of the larger stems and the growth rings counted by Dave Armstrong (NT). It was last pollarded around 153 years ago. It's not clear whether this was the first time it had been pollarded or if this would have been the last pollard in a long history of management of the tree.

Some notable dates: Pollarded - 1869.
Fastest, and quite consistent growth - 1892-1942.
Periods of noticeably slower growth - 1942-1947, 1952-57 and 1982-present.

The drought of 1976 doesn't appear to have had an immediate impact.

One of the elegant **silver birch** trees on the common in early spring.

Silver Birch

(Betula pendula)

Perhaps surprisingly given its delicate shape and slender branches, the birch is one of the hardiest of the broadleaf trees. It is native to much of the northern hemisphere, and can be found well above the arctic circle, where conditions are rather more severe than in our sheltered valley. At these higher latitudes, birch's only defence against storm and cold is to keep its head down and grow as a dwarf variety and will colonise areas that even the pines will not.

Birch is a deciduous, pioneer species being one of the first to grow in cleared or burnt areas, and isn't that fussy with soil or placement. It is said to have been one of the first species to appear in Britain at the end of the last ice age. Birch likes a lot of light, and manages that by being first off the grid wherever possible. Here in Sheepscombe you will find some growing in pairs on the slopes below the cricket ground, where, due to grazing and tree management they don't have any competition.

Bark is silver, papery & fissured

To those living in harsher climates and who rely (or used to rely) on firewood for their warmth, washing and cooking, birch is the ideal fuel tree. It is fast-growing and burns with a good heat, if a little fast. There's not much of this tree that can't be useful in some way. It lends itself to turning and carving, the bark is infused with natural oils that make it excellent tinder for lighting your log-burner*. Birch sap can be tapped in spring and is considered a 'superdrink' - tasting almost indistinguishable from water - and the twigs bundled together can make a brush or broom.

With its silvery-white bark and triangular 'ace of spades' shaped leaves, Birch is easily recognised and perhaps along with oak is one of the first trees we learn as children. There is often a single upright trunk with side branches becoming more slender along their length and giving way to even more delicate twigs. You may have spotted dense 'bird's nest' structures high in the crowns of some trees, but these are far from nests. They are called burelles, an over-exaggerated growth of twigs as a defence mechanism by the tree in response to an invasion of gall mite or fungus.

FIG. 55.—Birch.

1. Branch with Male and Female Catkins.
2. Female Flower.
3. Male Flower.   5. A Catkin in fruit.
4. Stamen.   6. Fruit.

Birch doesn't produce heavy shade even in full leaf and the dappled light allows flowers and shrubs to thrive underneath and in turn this is good for bugs and insects.

In late summer, young male catkins start to appear. Both male and female grow on the same tree, the male catkin long and droopy, while the females stay within buds until spring, opening to stand proud of the twig. These grow plump and green once pollinated, changing to brown by autumn, when the catkins loosen up releasing their seeds to the wind.

In the UK we have other variants of Birch: Paper birch (Betula papyrifera), being more ornamental with its obviously peeling paper-thin bark, and Downy birch (Betula pubescens), whose leaf stems are hairy while those of the silver birch are not.

In folk-law, Birch is known as the 'Lady of the Woods' due to its delicate appearance, and being one of the first to leaf in the spring was known as the tree of inception, and associated with cleansing the old to make way for the new. In Beltane festivals birch twigs are often used to light the oak fires.

On a windy day, birch will talk to you. Choose one whose branches are moving energetically, find a smooth area of bark, press an ear tight to the trunk to get a good seal and listen. You should hear the sounds of tiny knockings and scratchings of the branches and twigs transferred down the trunk. Young ash with its smooth bark is good for this too. Our beeches are too solid and huge for the sounds to propagate well.

Of course us reserved Brits don't tend to approve of those uninhibited Scandinavians who leap from their saunas naked into the snow and beat each other with birch twigs. Do we?

* If you do want to take birch bark as tinder or kindling it's best to do it responsibly from fallen logs or sparingly from the living tree where it's already peeling, so as not to damage it.

Blackthorn (Prunus spinosa)
Hawthorn (Crataegus monogyna)

These two companions of the hedgerow each have their own way of announcing that winter has finally let go of the Sheepscombe valley. In early spring you will notice that on each side of our narrow lanes things start greening up nicely, and that every so often splashes of delicate white blossom appear from bare spiky branches. It is hawthorn providing the green in early spring, and blackthorn the white.

Both species are remarkably useful to the farmer - and gardener - for hedgerows and barriers, as they both grow tangled, spiky and impenetrable, and are capable of holding back livestock. But what is an annoyance to sheep, cattle and foxes is a haven for mice, voles, rabbits, birds and insects who welcome the shade and safety that the prickly hedge corridors provide.

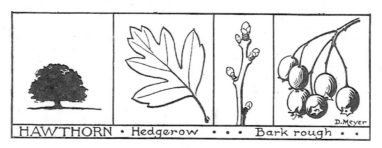

HAWTHORN · Hedgerow · · · Bark rough · ·

Motorways are often lined with alternating plantings of hawthorn and blackthorn so as to provide a long-lasting and attractive barrier to larger mammals straying where they shouldn't.

Blackthorn - part of the rose family - is usually the first to flower and does so before its leaves unfurl, and at its peak every inch of its outer twigs seem to be covered by simple white flowers, often appearing singly or in pairs along the length.

Hawthorn sensibly waits until its leaves are out before adding the blossom - possibly so as not to confuse the onlooker - by which time the blackthorn flowers are over and it now begins to show its green.

Both have near identical flowers - 5 small petals with delicate stamens, each flower on a short stalk. The hawthorn's group together in clusters - and you'll

Hawthorn: In full bloom and early growth. Lobed leaves, short spikes. Flowers after leaves (upper and left)

Blackthorn on the path above the pub: Oval toothed eaves, long spines and flowers before leaves (lower and right).

J Jones

34

see them against the leaves - whereas the blackthorn's gather in ones and twos on bare branches. Buds in both types appear alternate along branches and are small and brown, growing at an angle. In blackthorn the buds grow along those spines too.

The hawthorn berries - the haws - appear green soon after the flowers have withered and by autumn have turned deep red and hang in long-stalked bunches. These are eagerly devoured by fieldfares and redwings especially and thus the hard-cased seeds are spread around. The blackthorn fruit is the blue/purple sloe - of gin-flavouring fame and is ripe in early autumn.

Key identifiers are leaf shape and spines - see illustrations - the hawthorn leaf is multi-lobed with a toothed edge, while blackthorn is oval with a finer toothed edge. The spines in hawthorn grow out short and sharp from near the leaf base, whereas in blackthorn the spikes are longer and often have buds along their length.

It's worth noting that contrary to popular belief, the blackthorn's spines are not themselves poisonous, but that the wound produced is often deeper than the hawthorn and if left un-cleaned can become septic.

Glastonbury thorn (photo: wiki commons)

The UK's most famous hawthorn is the Holy Thorn of Glastonbury. Legend has it that Joseph of Arimathea arrived in Glastonbury with a few disciples and two vessels containing the blood and sweat of Jesus. He is said to have thrust his staff into the ground - it sprouted and became a thorn tree. The tree's descendants are still believed to stand on the hill. This particular hawthorn is said to bloom twice a year 'biflora', once in May and again around Christmas.

A sprig of one of these Glastonbury thorns from outside St Johns Church, was traditionally sent to the Queen at Christmas. Sadly the famous bush was vandalised in 2010.

Of course hawthorn is known as the May tree, and we have the famous adage: "Ne'er cast a clout 'till May be out", warning us not to put away our winter clothes until the hawthorn flowers. Time will tell if global warming puts paid to this lovely saying.

Blackthorn has a more sinister reputation in folklore, certainly in Irish tradition, as it was associated the the Cailleach, the goddess of winter, often portrayed as a twisted blue-veiled old woman, blackthorn staff in-hand. With this she was said to create mountains, lakes and valleys, as well as snow-storms and inclement weather.

Again in Ireland blackthorn is used to make shillelaghs, once a lethal weapon - a cross between a walking stick and a club. Designed to be able to passed off as one but able to be used as the other should the need arise!

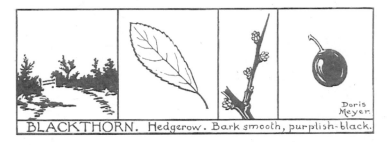

BLACKTHORN. Hedgerow. Bark smooth, purplish-black.

Fortunately I don't think we're troubled by highwaymen or footpads in Sheepscombe these days.

Irish shillelagh (photo: gad.net)

Catalpa
(*Catalpa bignoioides*)

This is a striking tree in many ways. It has huge heart-shaped leaves, attractive bell-shaped upright flower-clusters and a broad, spreading habit giving a lovely dappled shade. Fruits are long thin bean-like pods which often hang on through into winter and which give it the name 'Indian bean tree'.

This example provides spectacle and shade in a garden on Longridge. The species is a deciduous import, originally from south-

eastern USA and it is thought that the name comes from the the Cherokee Indian name "Kut-uhl-pah."

It comes into leaf later in the season than most in northern climates, and the flowers only appear after the leaves are fully grown. (Other trees with large heart-shaped leaves are foxglove tree, mulberry and broad-leaved lime). Leaves fall early and can leave a mulchy mess.

Unusually, catalpa leaves secrete nectar from pores located at the axils of the major veins (where these join the central vein). Ladybirds and ants are attracted by the insects that come for the sticky sweetness.

The pods (H Zell - Wiki)

In the southern USA at least, it is also known as the 'fish-bait tree' due to the 3" catalpa sphinx moth caterpillars - 'catalpa worms' that feed on its leaves. Children are sent to collect as many of these as possible for local fishermen.

Where plentiful, catalpa produces a durable hardwood, used for carving or turning, and for fence-posts where its rot-resistance is valued.

(This tree is on private land)

The **catalpa** or Indian bean tree in
a garden on Longridge.

Cedar of Lebanon

(Cedrus libani)

There's a Biblical character up on the bend in the track near the Ebworth Centre, amusingly opposite the Spirit of the Woods carving.

It is 990 BCE, ten centuries before the birth of Christ. King Solomon is looking for suitable timber to clad the lavish temple he is building for the worship of Yahweh and to hold the Ark of the Covenant. He is not impressed with the cypress and pine that he is being offered locally, and so turns to his friend Hiram the king of Tyre for a supply of cedar from Sidon (now southern Lebanon).

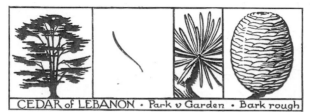

CEDAR of LEBANON • Park v Garden • Bark rough

Cedar wood is fragrant and a rich red before it weathers and so must have been an ideal choice, it's also easy to work, and resilient to rot and insects. You won't be surprised to know that it is still prized for these characteristics today.

Cedar is a source of an essential oil similar to turpentine and is used to make some cough medicines, ointments and antiseptic.

The Ancient Egyptians used it in the mummification process, with other essential oils such as thyme and peppermint. It is said to symbolise protection, wisdom and abundance and is used as incense and for clearing. Native Americans in their spiritual practise, reduce anger and promote positive feelings. Due to its high concentration of resin, cedar is great as kindling, but spits and burns too fast to be a useful wood-fuel.

This majestic evergreen can grow up to 35m although this one is more like 20m tall. Bark is blackish-brown with horizontal and vertical cracks. Distinctive features are wide sweeping branches with little clumps of needles along the

The magnificent but truncated **cedar of Lebanon** and admirer, opposite the Spirit of the Woods carving near the Ebworth Centre.

Western red cedar - *(thuja plicata)*

Interestingly, just the other side of the carving there is a perfectly conical western red cedar, probably another deliberate planting. Although actually not a true cedar, it is used in very similar ways for buildings and essential oils. It has very dense and low-growing foliage (used in hedging and screening), and if you look closely at the shoots, they are neither needle nor leaf, but a collection of scales. These give off a sweet smell if crushed .

length growing on short stubs. Male cones are large (8-12 cm high) and papery with a flattish, dimpled top, grow upright on the branch, and are produced every other year. Female cones are green/purple changing to brown as they mature, up to 12 months after pollination. This is a monoecious species (both male and female parts found on the same tree).

From the 18th century onwards, this statuesque and graceful tree was planted in the grounds of nearly every stately home and mansion, its sweeping branches no doubt providing shade for many an elegant picnic or dalliance.

This specimen is impressive but a little atypical, with no low branches - having to compete with close neighbours for light - and at some point has lost her crown, maybe from lightning strike. It's not clear when this was planted, but Gillian Hopkins told me "John Workman disliked conifers, because they were mostly non-native, and they killed off the under-storey plants. He only planted English larch as nursery trees. I think John said his father planted it to mark 1900, or perhaps the end of World War One."

As the trees age, owls and bats can make use of the large cracks and crevices that can appear, and their height makes them a good vantage point for hunting. There do appear to be a couple of hollows in the upper dead section of trunk which could be owl nests.

At the base of this one you can't fail to notice a metre-high pile of cedar needles and soil up against the trunk, and although there are no visible outer signs (after all we were in the depths of winter) this is a massive ants nest, built over the years by industrious workers, one needle at a time. That's quite a temple.

The **wild cherry** and daffodils by the road at Magpie Bottom.

Cherry (wild, bird)

(Prunus avium, padus)

Right on the bend coming into the village at Magpie Bottom, there's a tall broad tree that in spring glows whiter than a washing powder advert. In our part of the world at least, these are the first white flowers of spring, closely followed by blackthorn. It's easily mistaken for blackthorn especially in smaller bush form, the main difference being the lack of spikes on the cherry.

Also known as gean cherry, this tree is prized by gardeners, birds and woodworkers alike. The fruits it produces are rather small and sour, and it is

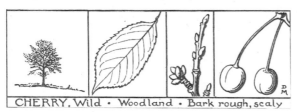

CHERRY. Wild · Woodland · Bark rough, scaly

only its descendant, the cultivated variety that produce the sweet ones we buy in punnets, and most of these come from Spain, Turkey or the US.

The ornamental cherry with heavy pink or white flowers is a particularly attractive sight in our parks and gardens, the tree is smaller and more spreading than the 'wild', and the bark often shinier and smoother.

Cherry belongs to the prunus family, whose other relatives include rose, blackthorn, bird and ornamental cherry, cherry laurel and damson - the leaves' serrated edges are a common trait to all these.

Buds are reddish-brown, alternate in pattern, around 1cm long and pointed. Flowers are on long stalks, white and with five petals. Cherry is an hermaphrodite, with both male and female parts in the same flower. Leaves are oval, pointed with serrated edges and up to 15cm long. The bark is quite easily identifiable - brown smooth and shiny, which is prone to peeling horizontally and shows circular pores or lenticles.

It is a popular source of food for birds, who are involved of course in the distribution of the stones - this is where the 'avium' comes from. We can eat the fruits, but they can be quite sour and beware, the stones are poisonous in quantity - they contain small traces of cyanide.

For wood-turners and cabinet-makers, cherry wood is a delight. Once cut and seasoned (slowly to prevent warping) and with exposure to the sun - the wood, which starts with a salmon hue, begins to take on the rich red tone that we associate with cherry.

 Colonial furniture makers are said to have called cherry "New England mahogany" because of its tendency to turn dark red-brown after exposure to sunlight. The heartwood is rather darker than the younger sapwood. It is especially favoured for the way it takes cutting, shaping and sanding, and is a very dense, hard wood.

Beware the cherry phantom! If you leave anything like a lamp or a book obstructing the light on newly-made cherry furniture for any great length of time, the wood underneath your object will not darken as fast as the rest and you will be left with a mark that may never disappear.

As a firewood, cherry is not as good a performer as ash or oak, but does burn with a pleasant aroma.

Essence of sour cherry such as Montmorency, has been used as a flavouring in foods and in medicine since olden times and is anecdotally linked to several health benefits, including boosting the immune system, improving memory, and aiding sleep.

Just around the curve there's a row of **Bird Cherry** (Prunus padus) trees . They are easy to spot because bird cherry's leaves are more elongated than its wild cousin, and the flowers hang down on a vertical stem rather than all come out from a single point. In spring, the blooms have a powerful almond-like scent attracting hordes of insects.

After pollination the flowers develop into small sour reddish-black berries. These trees are reasonably rare in the south west of the UK, but where they're found they tend to favour wet woodland, hedgerows and stream and river banks.

(These trees are on private land - but are visible from the road)

Bird cherry. The five-petalled flowers hang on short stalks while those of wild cherry grow out from the same point. The leaves are oval and pointed with fine serrations. Fruits are inedible.

Japan comes to Sheepscombe in a garden on Longridge.

Below, a panorama of **Yoshino** and **Accolade** with Painswick behind. Right, flowers of **Mikinori**.

The **metasequoia** in the garden at Church
Orchard in spring, planted by John Workman
in 1951.

Dawn Redwood - Metasequoia
(*Metasequoia glyptostroboides*)

I don't wish to alarm you, but we have right here in the village nothing less than a living fossil. At around 15m tall, this specimen lives in the garden at Church Orchard next to the pub, and fortunately for us seems to have no desire to stray. Once thought to be extinct, this is no woolly mammoth or dinosaur but instead goes by the more reassuring common name of dawn redwood.

Leaf prints of this ancient tree exist in the fossil record from Mesozoic times (65 to 250 million years ago) but it was only in the 1940s - a mere blink of the eye in geological time - that a group of hitherto unknown deciduous conifers were discovered by Chinese botanists near the Yangtze river. These matched known fossils and were later identified as a new living species after the war.

North Korean postage stamp of a fossil Metasequoia leaf.

This caused quite a stir, and in short order the Arnold Arboretum of Harvard University sent an expedition to collect seeds and subsequently, seedlings were distributed to various universities and arboreta worldwide for growth trials. It has since proved very popular in parks, arboretums and larger gardens in temperate climates. It is on the endangered list, and is especially vulnerable in its native China where much has been lost to logging.

This tree was planted in 1951 by John Workman from a seedling brought from Kew Gardens by the then owner of Church Orchard, William Newman, who worked there. A fast grower, this one put on much of its height between 1951 and 1997 although it seems to have slowed since.

The bark and foliage is very similar to its cousin sequoia, but Metasequoia is deciduous with its needle-like leaves turning a rich golden brown in autumn.

Dawn redwood shows generally a conical shape, dominated by a straight, tapering, fluted and characterful trunk with fibrous bark, and which shows distinctive 'armpits' under the side branches. Leaves are opposite and 1-3 cm long, bright green and fern-like.

The pollen cones are 5–6 mm long, and appear in early spring; they are produced only on trees growing in regions with hot summers. The female cones are roughly ovoid, 1.5–2.5 cm and they mature some 8–9 months after pollination. It is monoecious with both male and female parts on the same tree.

Metasequoia will grow in most situations, and thrives best in deep loamy moist soils but will even cope with growing in standing water. Indeed one of the early specimens identified in China formed part of a local shrine, where villagers called it Shui-shan or "water fir".

Growing as it does, only metres away from the equally ancient ginkgo on the corner by the pub, one can only wonder what they both make of the modern world and if they discuss life back then on Pangea[2].

Male pollen cones among the foliage. (photo: Wiki commons)

(This tree is on private land but is just visible from the road. There are two others in the valley below the first pond in Workmans Wood)

[1] nationaltrust.org.uk//the-ebworth-centre
[2] a supercontinent that existed during the late Paleozoic and early Mesozoic eras

Metasequoia's trunk is very characterful, fluted and flaky with age and especially fissured where branches emerge.

Elder in bloom by the school and a black elder bush at Greycot. Each head of flowers is held flat to catch the most sun and entice the most insects.

Elder

(Sambucus nigra)

I realise that I have been avoiding elderberry for some time now. Why should that be? Maybe I was too focused on beech, pine and oak - tall and strong. Or seduced by birch, willow or aspen - slender and attractive. Shallow observer! I was overlooking the many gifts that she has to offer.

It's true, elder presents a rather untidy sight, living as she often does on waste-ground or by the roadside, branches all over the place. The wood is brittle, light and pithy and of no use on log fires. But in folk-law, if oak is the King and beech is the Queen of the woodlands, then elder is the wise woman, the stern grandmother, the Elder.

But what she may lack in looks, she makes up for in bounty. In late spring we collect her densely packed white flowery heads for cordial, wine or tea.

Those that remain, will in the autumn produce deep purple berries, offering the chance to make cordials or wine, rich in vitamin C and iron. The flowers and berries are mildly poisonous so must be cooked before eating. Once the pith is drilled and the stems dried they can become simple flutes or whistles or be used to blow a reluctant fire to life.

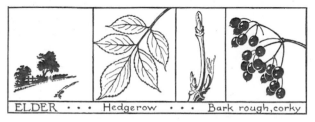

ELDER · · · Hedgerow · · · Bark rough, corky

Distinctive features of elder are the pinnate leaf construction, each comprising 5-7 oval leaflets with tiny serrations around the edge. Look out for a shrub or small tree with haphazard branch growth and in season, the classic flower heads - umbels - are cleverly designed to present the tiny white flowers on a nearly flat surface to the sun (like cow-parsley). Bark is grey-brown and corky getting more furrowed with age.

A variety of insects love the flowers for the nectar, and the berries are eaten by birds and mammals alike. Moth caterpillars feed on the leaves, including the white-spotted pug, swallowtail, dot moth and buff ermine.

Herbalists tell us that an elderflower tea helps to bring on a cleansing sweat to combat cold and 'flu-like symptoms, and elderberry drinks can be prescribed as an anti-viral.

It was believed that elder by your front door would keep evil spirits from entering the house, and that anyone standing under an elder on mid-summer's eve would be able to see the faery-folk, but don't fall asleep or you'll be carried off! So I've missed that dead-line. Next year maybe.

Green Elder Salve For sprains, strains, aches and bruises. Don't use on broken skin. This recipe makes a green ointment for external healing. Fresh elder stems and leaves can be toxic if taken internally.

- Pick elder leaves in mid-summer when they are fresh, whole, green and full of vitality. Shred and leave to wilt for a couple of hours. Place in a Pyrex dish and cover with an organic oil, (sunflower, rapeseed or olive) and cover loosely with foil or place the lid on the dish at an angle without securing it, this allows any water vapour to escape.

- Put this dish into a bain maire (tin filled with water at least half way up the sides of the glass dish) and put into your oven on the lowest heat. Leave for 2-3 hours, checking the water level occasionally. The oil will turn a rich dark green. Strain. If you see any water droplets in the oil, allow these to separate and decant the oil off to remove this water.

- Add beeswax in a ratio of 1 part beeswax to 8 parts oil, warm gently till the beeswax melts. Fill your jars that have been cleaned and sterilised. You can add drops of essential oils to the oil/wax blend (10-20 drops per 50ml) just before filling the jars, for a pleasant scent. Ginger and rosemary essential oils are beneficial additions as they promote circulation to the damaged tissues, supporting healing. Allow to cool and set.

Julie Wood www.wildhealinggarden.co.uk

It's been a slow start, but I've learnt that elder is a very potent native, to be respected and listened to, like grandma.

English or Common Elm

(Ulmus procera)

I had pretty much given up looking for elm, so devastating has Dutch elm disease been to the population, and we must have walked nearly every path in the valley. So I was delighted to learn that one was alive and relatively well, just 30m along from the school. Another character hiding in plain sight! It stands probably 15m tall right by the side of the road along with a number of shoots in the nearby hedge.

This one is rather spindly, having had to cope with competition from the trees in the bank behind and the chain-saws of the electricity company carving a route for our power lines.

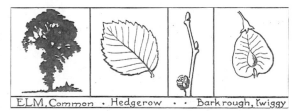

ELM, Common • Hedgerow • • Bark rough, twiggy

Looking for some insight into their abundance before they were blighted, I turned to a book from 1938 that belonged to the grandmother of dear family friends. Actually written for children it opens a poignant window into the elms of those times, so I thought I would let the authors speak directly to us[1]:

~ Some girls and boys will no doubt have their favourite trees, as we have, and the Elm is one of these, probably because we see this tree every day and thus get to know it so well. Yet the Common Elm is not a native of Britain, like its lesser-known cousin the Wych Elm, ... Some people say that the Romans brought it to England. This may or may not be true, but it is a fact that the Roman sites that we have ourselves seen, have Elm trees not far away.

The Elm loves hedgerows and lanes, and in March or April the bare look of winter gives place to a glow of life produced by the tufts of dense, reddish-brown flowers spread along the Elm's branches. These flowers appear in advance of the leaves, and before one has time to realise what is happening - the small seeds, winged all round, are to be seen. These gather strength as they become larger, and at last there are great bunches of them in a good season.

The seed is towards the top of the winged fruit - called a samara - and in spite of their great number they very rarely ripen. Clouds of them are very often seen blowing away from the tree in late May and June. They are almost white, and about the size of a three-penny-bit to a sixpence.

The **English elm** by the road on Far End lane. Small serrated leaves, rough to feel, with an asymmetric base. Rough, fissured bark.

The short-stalked alternate leaves vary in size and shape, one lobe being lower down the leaf-stalk than the other. They have pointed ends and are toothed.

Fig. 32.—Common Elm in Winter; on right, a Winter Twig.

[Common elm leaves are smaller than wych elm and have a less pronounced asymmetry] Elm normally sheds its leaves early, the autumn tint being yellow-lemon to pale gold.

It is a taller and less spreading tree than the Wych. It has a rough, corky bark with deep furrows, and produces abundant suckers. The wood is heavy and tough, and is used for many purposes.

It has several enemies - including the Elm bark beetle - and even when not attacked a healthy limb may snap off during the quiet of a summer's day. This habit of shedding branches gives its crown an uneven shape, with big clusters of leaves unequally spaced by the gaps they leave. The foliage is very thick in summer, while in winter the numerous fine twigs and small buds have a delicate lacy appearance against the sky. The Wych Elm has a broader crown. ~

Dutch elm disease in its most virulent form, hit our shores in 1967. First identified by Dutch scientists, but probably brought over on logs from N. America, more than 25 million trees died in the UK, and by 1990 very few mature elms were left here or in the rest of Europe. It is a fungal disease spread by elm bark beetles, and kills the tree by blocking its vascular system. These beetles - Scolytus scolytus - only tend to attack mature trees over 20 years old. Their larvae tunnel into the bark and outermost wood layers, carrying the fungus, which infects the tree and is carried by newly-hatched beetles as they fly to the next one. Elm can reproduce through suckers, but these are not immune either and most will succumb to the fungus as they mature. (forestresearch.gov.uk)

Having spent longer with elm now, she comes across as a tough-skinned and taut customer. Resilient even, as I guess she has to be.

(This tree is on private land - but it is visible from the road)

[1]Look and Find Out about Trees - W P Westell & Kate Harvey - Macmillan & Co

The majestic and finely balanced **eucalyptus** in the garden at Pinetops on Longridge.

Eucalyptus

(Eucalyptus spp)

Kookaburra sits in the old gum tree? Staring up at this lofty specimen against a clear blue sky in the garden at Pinetops, you could imagine any number of exotic Australian birds and even a dozy koala in the branches, and be transported to the banks of the Darling river rather than the slopes of Longridge.

Although naturalised in the UK, this is of course a native of Australia, where it is widespread in all but the most arid areas of the country. It is a distinctive, lanky evergreen with large bunches of blue-grey leaves that are slender and pointed when mature, but start out life smaller and rounded. The classic bark is a flakey blue-grey and yellowish where it has peeled off.

Immature leaves

Flower buds are presented in groups of three on short stalks and are cone-shaped. Each bud has a round cap on top - the calyptus, and this falls off to reveal the fluffy white or red flower stamens, that are very attractive to bees. Flowers give way to a woody pod that opens to release seeds.

Indigenous Australians held the eucalyptus as holy and used nearly all parts of the tree. Leaves and leaf oils were used for their medicinal properties and as a healing tea, and the sap (the gum) used as an adhesive resin. The timber and bark would be made into tools, spears, shields and musical instruments and is still used in large-scale construction, furniture-making and as pulpwood. Water carriers - tarnuks - were made from a hollowed-out burl of eucalyptus and certain communities made canoes from the bark (see box).

We still use the leaf-oils today; in aromatherapy, as a inhalation decongestant, a chest rub to help clear mucus and sooth coughs, and as an insect repellant. Unfortunately for the often tinder-dry outback, eucalyptus oil is highly flammable and this exacerbates the bush-fires that ravage the countryside from time to time.

The bark canoes of Australia's Murray river. These canoes were formed from a single piece of bark of the river red gum tree (Eucalyptus camaldulensis). A man would climb a tree and cut a lozenge-shaped section of bark, using either a stone axe or sharpened sticks. On occasion -- especially where the bark being taken was high on the tree -- the builder would cut hand- and toe-holds as an aid to climbing.

Flat, flexible sticks were pressed between the bark and the wood all around the cut, being forced in bit by bit. Before the bark came away from the trunk, a line was passed around it to prevent it from falling to the ground. (The wood of the river red gum, by the way, is too dense to serve as a good dugout canoe, and even the bark is somewhat difficult to work.)

A tree from which a section of bark has been cut for a canoe.

Once flat on the ground, small sticks were placed under the bark to support its perimeter edges and small fires were built on top to evaporate much of the sap. This also caused the centre to sag down, increasing the curvature of the hull and the height of the sides. A few sticks were placed across the hull from sheer to sheer to prevent the bark from curling inward too far, and sometimes these were left in place, in the nature of thwarts, when construction was complete.

Text from Bob Hotzman's blog: indigenousboats.blogspot.com by kind permission.

It seems that the tree was first brought over to the UK in the 1770s from one of Cook's expeditions - it was at this time that the name eucalyptus was coined, derived from the Greek 'eu' and 'calyptus', meaning 'well' and 'covered', referring to the cap that protects the developing flower parts.

For the original peoples of Australia this tree represents the division of the underworld, Earth and heaven. They hold that you can disperse negative energy by burning the leaves.

It is also said that if there is gold in the ground under its roots, then eucalyptus will absorb this and exude it out of its leaves. No wonder kookaburra is laughing.

(This tree is on private land - but is visible from the road)

False acacia - Black Locust *(Robinia pseudoacaia)*
Ginkgo - Maidenhair tree *(Ginkgo biloba)*

Two exotic species this month*, having come to us from opposite sides of the globe. The first can be seen 80 yards up the track at Magpie Bottom while the other is visible every time we step out of the pub. False acacia is a native of the eastern USA while ginkgo has come to us from the Far East.

Also known as the black locust, **false acacia** first appeared in the UK in the late 1800s. It is characterised by a deeply fissured trunk, on older specimens,

with deciduous compound leaves with 5 to 11 pairs of leaflets either side of the stem (pinnate). A pair of thorns grows where the main leaf stalk meets the twig. In late spring large volumes of fragrant white pea-like flowers appear, which bees love. Later in the year, dark brown pea-like pods are produced and these hang on well into winter. You may not be surprised to learn that it is a part of the pea family.

In addition to being a prolific seeder, false acacia is also adept at putting down suckers and this is one of its disadvantages as far as humans are concerned as

if left unattended it will produce thickets and suckers pop up all over the place. It's a fast grower partly because it fixes its own nitrogen into the soil and is thus good at colonising poor soils.

In North America it is prone to attack by the locust borer, a type of longhorn beetle, but it is unclear who gave who the name. Original Americans prized the wood for their bows, while white settlers found it to be an excellent building material, hard and rot-resistant. These days in the US, where it is more prolific it is used to make garden tool-handles and outdoor furniture.

The open canopy allows lots of light through which encourages smaller plants and bushes to thrive underneath. False acacia makes good firewood and

False acacia in Magpie Bottom
(above) & **ginkgo** by the pub (below).

burns very hot. There are three examples in Magpie Bottom, now about 15m tall which were planted from seed around 1987.

The **ginkgo** is the only living example of the division Ginkgophyta, an ancient tree species found in fossils in China dating back 270 million years and will have been around in the age of the dinosaurs. Until only a couple of hundred years ago it was thought to be extinct, but unknown to the West it had survived in Chinese monasteries and temple gardens. It later spread to Japan from where seeds were brought to Europe in the early C18[th] .

A deciduous tree growing up to 25m which develops an irregular, spreading crown as it ages. Ginkgo has attractive fan-shaped, 2-lobed leaves that are spirally arranged on long stems, green in the summer and turning yellow in autumn.

Ginkgo leaves with male catkins

Male trees - the most common - have yellow catkins up to 8cm long and produce the pollen, while female trees grow two ovules at the end of stalks. Green at first, these yellow with age and have a pungent smell.

The name ginkgo comes from the Chinese 'yinxing' meaning 'silver apricot' and was named the maidenhair tree in the UK because the leaves look similar to our native maidenhair fern.

To the ancient Chinese, the tree was a manifestation of the sacred concept of yin and yang, a symbol of longevity and vitality and believed to be beneficial for those with circulation or memory problems, and is still a popular herbal remedy today. Many Daoist temple courtyards feature ancient gingko trees that may be thousands of years old.

So next time you step out of the pub, do have a word with the tree that was once food for dinosaurs.

(These trees are on private land - but you can see them from the road)

*These articles were originally published monthly in the Sheepscombe News

The Village Hall **field maple** in late summer and its five-fingered 'palmate' leaves, here in spring.

Classic winged helicopter seeds ready for wind or child distribution.

Field Maple
(Acer Campestre)

Once a year, the normally reserved field maple puts on a lovely show. You may well have spotted the glorious gold that shoots through its compact, lobed leaves each autumn before our valley winds blows them all away.

Field maple is the Uk's only native maple and is well-adapted to our rural farming landscape and most often found in southern England. You'll spot it either in the wood-edge or occupying our hedgerows, sometimes standing proud, escaping the wrath of the hedge-cutter, or joining in the scrum of the hedge itself. In towns it is also a favourite as it tolerates pollution well, doesn't grow too big and is popular for its autumn display.

When allowed to grow to maturity it rarely reaches more than 8-10m tall, with a short trunk, a rounded crown and is densely branched. It is also happy being a large shrub, with multiple stems.

It provides a rich habitat and feeding ground for aphids and moth caterpillars, and therefore also to their predators: ladybirds, hoverflies and birds. The flowers provide nectar and pollen for bees, and small mammals visit for the fruit.

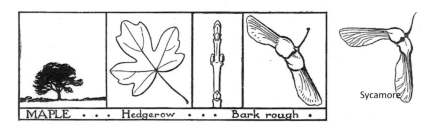

MAPLE . . . Hedgerow . . . Bark rough . Sycamore

A relative of the sycamore (Acer pseudoplatanus) and Norway maple (Acer platanoides), field maple has the smaller leaves, with five rounded palmate lobes. Next in size is Norway maple with its very 'pointy' lobed leaves with each lobe having parallel sides. Sycamore has the biggest leaves of the three, but they are not as pointed as Norway maple and often show 'tar spot', a fungal growth.

A good indicator of all maples is that they grow opposing buds along the stem. The flowers are hermaphrodite - having both male and female reproductive parts within the one flower - and are small, yellow-green, cup-shaped and hang in clusters.

After pollination the flowers develop into winged fruits - the classic 'helicopter' - dispersed by the wind. Field maple's wings are set in a nearly straight line whereas sycamore's are more of a 90 degree angle.

On established trees the bark exhibits a wavy rippled surface, whilst younger stems in a hedge or coppiced are much smoother. It is fast growing and as we have learnt, bears clipping well into a hedge.

There's not a great deal of mythology or symbolism associated with field maple. In Europe it used to be said that branches could prevent bats from entering a house, and renowned 17th Century herbalist Nicholas Culpeper thought that the leaves and bark were good for the liver.

Maple wood has been used for centuries for carving, for veneers and in violin and harp making, where the 'tone' of the wood and the effect of various layers of lacquer or varnish are critical. Generally the back, ribs, neck and scroll of a violin are of maple (a hardwood), while the belly - the front - is of spruce (a softwood).

The sap is slightly sugary and like all maples, can be boiled down to make maple syrup - trees are tapped in the spring when the sap is rising. But before anyone starts stalking the few Sheepscombe maples for syrup, it's worth knowing that it is the 'sugar maples' from Canada that are the ones producing the varieties you see on the shelves.

photo: spidlen.com

Besides which if the Parish Council were to catch you, it would surely be a bitter-sweet experience.

Guelder Rose

(*Viburnum opulus*)

Ok it's not a tree, but this flamboyant shrub is well worth seeking out in your wanderings around the valley. Nor is it a rose, and the name originated in the Dutch province of Gelderland, where it is said they used to grow snowball trees, a cultivar. Once you know what to look for it's pretty easy to spot at any time of the year. Right now (February), it is bare and pale and identified by twigs growing opposite from the stem.

Leaves are quite distinctive with three lobes, indented veins visible from the upper surface and a layer of hairs on the underside. Don't confuse it with a young sycamore or field maple which also have symmetrical twigs and rather similar leaf shapes if different sizes. In winter it can be confused with elder, but the latter grows much more untidily and with multiple stems. Guelder prefers damp conditions and is also referred to as swamp or water elder, being in the same family.

In early summer you will see branched clusters of creamy-white, flat-topped flowers. Unusually each spray of small fertile flowers is encircled by a ring of larger, sterile flowers, whose job it is to attract pollinators to the plant. In autumn, bunches of bright red berries appear, these often remain after the leaves have turned red and fallen, and are favourites of bullfinch, mistle thrush and fieldfare.

The dried bark is used by herbalists in a tincture, known as "cramp bark," to alleviate menstrual pains and other muscle tension and spasms. The berries are bitter and mildly toxic if taken in quantity, but made into a jelly, the bitterness disappears into sweetness. I have heard that your kitchen may

Part of the **guelder rose** enclave 100m into
Workmans Wood, by the enclosure. Berries, flowers and distinctive leaf shape.

smell of old socks for a while - but don't be put off! When dried, the berries turn black and were once used for making ink.

Various Slavic cultures have association with guelder. In Ukrainian folklaw the berries symbolize home and native land, blood, and family roots. In Russia the fruit is called 'kalina' and is a national symbol. Kalina can mean "to make red-hot". The red fiery colour representing female beauty but the bitter taste reminding us of separation and loss.

So beware, gentle summer traveller of woodland paths, lest you tarry too long and taste too deeply of the inviting red fruits.

~~~~

A view from the common, looking south across the village to Blackstable Woods, with hazel in the foreground.

Spring **hazel** with catkins on the Hillcot path, Far End.

Hazel

(*Corylus avellana*)

You need only venture a few steps up above the gardens of Sheepscombe to find yourself in a belt of hazel that later gives way to the beeches and conifers higher up. Hazel's distinctive golden catkins (lamb's tails) are one of the early signs of spring.

A deciduous species, hazel is borderline between shrub and tree because it grows with multiple trunks like a shrub (rarely more than 6 to 10 m tall), but each trunk can become fairly thick and woody like a tree.

Its presence on the slopes of our valley in such quantity is largely due to its suitability for coppicing in the past (see text box over). It does like lots of light and so is hardly ever found under our dense canopies of beech.

Hazel is monoecious (meaning that both male and female parts exist on the same individual). The catkins are male and enlarge recognisably from their small brown winter shape as they fill with pollen in late January or early February. The female parts are small and bud-like with groups of thin red strands or styles.

Hazel flowers must be pollinated by pollen from a different tree and the resultant oval fruits appear in late spring, hanging in groups of one to four.

By autumn they mature into the famous nuts with a woody shell surrounded by a cup of leafy bracts, just in time for burying by local squirrels or harvesting for a certain french nutty chocolate spread.

The leaf is a pointed oval/heart shape 5-10cm long with serrated edges, and goes from a lime-green in the the spring through

by Sophie Marley: blogs.reading.ac.uk

rich mid-green in summer to brown tints in the autumn. The leaves can stay on the tree longer than most, often into December, by which time they are yellow. The bark tends to be smooth and silvery-brown and speckled with lenticles, the pores of the tree.

Coppicing involves cutting the tree down to just above ground level, and allowing shoots to grow up from within or around the the remaining stump or stool. These fast-growing stems (benefiting from strong existing roots and the extra light) are allowed to grow for a number of years, dependant on what final use the wood is to be put to - poles, fencing, firewood or charcoal for example. Depending on the wood, a pole say for a walking stick might take 3 - 5 years to grow, whereas one suitable for a fence post might take 10 - 15 years.

A given woodland area can be sub-divided into sections or 'cants' and coppiced in rotation, to give a continuous supply of wood. Favourites for coppicing are: sweet chestnut, hazel, ash, hornbeam, willow and field maple. There are no signs that Sheepscombe hazel is worked anymore as all the individuals I have seen are overstood - left too long to their own devices. But throughout the woods there are many charcoal platforms to be found - often now inhabited by badgers - and traces of burnt wood are sometimes present under the leaf-litter.

The Celts regarded the hazel as the tree of knowledge. Ireland seems to have had the greatest affinity with the tree, and we are told of a King named Mac Coll, meaning 'Son of Hazel'. In the Triads of Ireland it is recorded that Coll (hazel) and Quert (apple), were the only two trees whose wanton felling carried the death penalty.

A hazel dowser - sussexliving.com

Hazel sticks have historically been used by those who practise dowsing, and in Wales hazel twigs were woven into 'wishing caps', supposed to grant the wishes of the wearer.

Hazel is so bendy in spring that it can be tied in a knot without breaking. Interestingly bees find it difficult to collect the pollen because it is not that sticky and grains actually repel one grain another.

As firewood, hazel burns quickly and doesn't spit, so it is probably most useful split up and dried for use as kindling.

Holly *(Ilex aquifolium)*
Yew *(Taxus baccata)*

Take a walk up through our glorious beechwoods in spring and summer and it won't escape your notice that the rather dominating canopy doesn't allow a great deal of light to filter downwards, and consequently not much grows underneath.

Nonetheless two evergreen species have made their home here and do seem to thrive in these dull conditions. Holly and yew (along with ivy and box) provide us with some of the only splashes of green to be found in the woods at this time of year.

Holly is a slow-growing bush/tree which tends to form a rather dense untidy conical shape, and can reach a height of 15m and live up to 300 years.

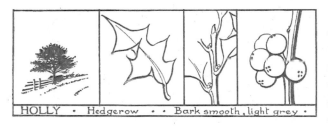

HOLLY • Hedgerow • • Bark smooth, light grey •

Interestingly the dark-green spiky leaves tend to get less aggressive the further up the tree they grow (safer from grazing cattle), although young shoots provide midwinter food for deer who seem to be able to cope with the spikes.

It is a white and dense wood, useful for turning, carving or making walking sticks. In the fireplace it burns well, even unseasoned, and gives a good heat.

Male and female flowers occur on different trees and it is the female that produces the red berries that are so sought after by birds for food or by us humans for Christmas decoration. If you were out and about in December looking for suitable clippings you may have disturbed a mistle-thrush bravely guarding the berries from other birds - and they are rather partial to yew berries too, but watch out - both are poisonous.

Holly flowers are white with four petals and appear from May onwards. Keep an eye out for the Holly Blue butterfly, whose caterpillar feeds on the blossoms.

An autumn **holly** bush in Lord's Wood.

A winter **yew** in Workmans Wood, in from St George's Field.

The Holly and the Ivy

Since pagan times the holly has been surrounded by superstition - the dark evergreen foliage coming to symbolize everlasting life. The leaves once formed part of the treatment for Smallpox as it was thought to relieve fevers.

The holly and ivy of Christmas carol fame is said to refer to a custom in pre-Christian times of dressing boys in a suit of holly leaves and girls in ivy, to symbolize nature passing through winter and into the fertility of spring. (Maybe it was thought too risky to dress children in poisonous yew.)

Yew is a long-lived conifer, with a reddish-brown flaky bark and soft needle-like leaves. It is often associated with Churchyards (St Mary's Painswick especially). Mature trees can grow up to 20m tall and the oldest recorded Yew is in Fortingall, Perthshire, said to be between 2000 and 3000 years old.

The dark green leaves are narrow, flattened and grow in opposite pairs. Underneath they are lighter with two yellow strips. Like the holly, male and

Yew tree bark, leaves and female aril.

female flowers grow on separate trees and are visible in March and April, when clouds of pollen are released at the slightest movement.

The male flower is yellow and the female, green. Both form at the leaf bases. Female flowers develop into a hard olive-green seed in a fleshy red cup (an aril). Both the leaves and the seed are poisonous to animals and humans.

Yew wood is fine grained, the dense heartwood being strong under compression and the sap-wood elastic and good under tension. These special properties meant that it was used in Medieval times to make the longbows that helped our English archers to victory, most famously in the battle of Agincourt in 1415.

Yew will grow quite thickly and is often clipped into decorative shapes (topiary) in parks or grand gardens.

St Mary's has around a hundred trees, clipped religiously twice a year. It is unclear why it is so prevalent in churchyards, but theories include planting there as a source of wood for longbows or that its poison protected the dead. They say that each time they try to count the yews, the number is different!

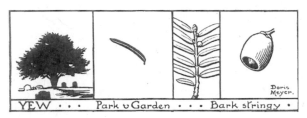

YEW · · · Park ʋ Garden · · · Bark stringy ·

The Romans believed that the yew grew in hell, Druids hold it sacred, whilst it is said that the Norse and Celt peoples believed that it protected against bewitchment and death.

Certainly yew's ability to root and then produce new saplings from drooping branches, along with it's longevity would lend itself to beliefs surrounding death and resurrection

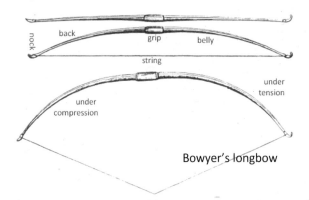

Bowyer's longbow

So whichever particular folk-law story you may or may not subscribe to, do give a passing nod to these two sturdy evergreen inhabitants of our woodlands as you pass them by.

Hornbeam

(Carpinus betulus)

With so much beech in our valley, it's easy to overlook the occasional hornbeam among our woods and hedgerows, as they can seem so similar at first glance. There are important differences however, not least of which that hornbeam is much less likely than beech to be dropping limbs on your head in a storm!

The big giveaway is that hornbeam has been working out. The trunk seems to be bursting with muscles twisting up the tree. As for the leaves, they are more deeply veined than beech with double-toothed edges, whereas beech's are wavy-edged.

Hornbeam's leaves grow alternately on the twig, with soft hairs on the underside, again like beech , so don't be fooled!

This month's specimen is growing in a garden on Longridge and is probably 20+ meters in height.

Colloquial names such as 'musclewood' and 'ironwood' give away the fact that hornbeam is a tough customer. Indeed 'horn' refers to the hardness of the wood and 'beam' is an old word for tree.

Fig. 60.—Hornbeam.

1. Branch with Male and Female Catkins.
2. Female Catkin in fruit.
3. Male Flower.   6. Female Flower.
4. Stamen.   7. Fruit.
5. Bract with two Female Flowers.

It's density means hornbeam is great for burning, and has long found itself in demand in applications of heavy use such as the cogs for water and windmills, the hubs of cartwheels or butcher's chopping blocks. It is hard to work and carpenters in the past were not always best pleased to be presented with this wood 'for his tools lose their edge far too quickly to be profitable'[1].

Hornbeam is monoecious (male and female parts are found on the same tree),

The **hornbeam** in a garden on Longridge.

Leaves similar to beech, but more heavily veined, and a fluted muscular trunk.

(from Westonbirt)

green catkins form in the spring and develop into long papery clusters of winged fruit (samaras) later in the year.

Hornbeam in hedges, like some beech, although deciduous, can keep its leaves on during winter, which affords some shelter to birds and small animals through the cold months. This quality can help you identify hornbeam when most others have dropped their leaves.

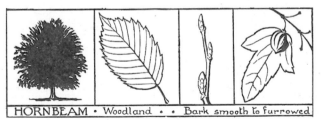

HORNBEAM • Woodland • • Bark smooth to furrowed

Herbalists have used the leaves in a tincture or a tea to soothe symptoms of coughs or colds, or crushed as a poultice to assist in wound healing. Not one for publicity, this tree is the strong and silent type.

(This tree is on private land)

[1]Wayside and Woodland trees - E Step - F Warne (1904)

~~~

A carpet of wild garlic on Elder Hill - photo Julie Wood

The **horse chestnut** under the bend by
Magpie Bottom. Seven palmate leaflets,
conker and panticle.

Horse Chestnut
(*Aesculus hippocastanum*)

Soak them overnight in vinegar? Bake them in the oven when mum was out, but remember to turn the oven off afterwards? Highlight of the autumn term, the horse chestnut trees outside my school would drop their spiky packages and there inside, gleaming burnished-brown would be the conker - and a potential winner. Perhaps a 'tenner' or even a 'twentyer', but hopefully not the ignominy of a 'noner'!

A few years ago it seemed that Councils wanted to ban the game, but it's not good to wrap our children in cotton wool and fortunately I believe that youngsters are once again allowed to bash the heck out of each other's prize specimens before the bell goes.

CHESTNUT, Horse • Pk. & Garden • Bark smooth to scaly

This is another easily recognised species with its palmate leaf structure of up to seven elongated serrated leaflets. In late spring, and depending on the variant, they will be decked in white or red flower 'candlesticks' or more properly panticles. In common with maples, sycamore, ash, dogwood and elder, horse chestnut buds are arranged in opposite pairs on the twig.

As winter hits, the tree now bare of leaves, reveals how its branches dip down and sweep up at the end, terminating in large sticky buds. This stickyness helps keep the 'scales' of the bud together as it grows, and may deter predators.

In spring, this sizeable package bursts open, allowing the leaves and flower bud within to unfurl. Later, the flower will produce the seed, the conker.

When the leaves fall from the twig, the scar left behind has a characteristic pattern of marks that resemble a horse shoe. This could be how the tree got its English name or perhaps because the conkers used to be made into

horse-feed, but we now believe they are mildly poisonous. Misnomers abound where this tree is concerned, because the seed is not related to the chestnut of sweet chestnut fame, which is edible.

Blights and bugs. Various agencies seem to conspire to have a go at the poor horse chestnut: *Leaf Blight* - appears as brown blotches and curling leaves, and often affects whole trees and their neighbours. This is a fungal infection probably exacerbated by a wet spring. Unfortunately the trees up near The Park have succumbed to leaf blight as seems more and more common these days.

Leaf Miner is a moth whose caterpillars eat tiny tunnels thorough the leaves, eventually killing them. *Bleeding Canker* is visible on the trunk as a brown secretion and is caused by a bacterial infection which if severe enough can kill the tree. Although unsightly, the leaf blight and miner moth don't seem to do lasting damage to the tree.

Native to Balkan forests, it was introduced to the UK in the late 16th century and has become popular on our streets, parks and estates. It needs a well-drained soil and good sun, but is fairly tolerant of soil type. The heart-wood is fine grained and creamy-white and used for veneers and for turning

This tree seems to be a healthy specimen, possibly due to its isolation from others. However, the owner has an intriguing theory that the power cables that pass through the crown of the tree - and may zap it from time to time - somehow confer an immunity from leaf blight. Village experts what do you think?

(This tree is on private land - but it is visible from the road)

Japanese maple

(Acer palmatum)

It's fully winter as I write this, the first snows are falling and suddenly there is no colour. But only yesterday it was autumn, and a week ago there were multiple colours clothing the valley including a stunning splash of orange visible across the valley from where we are.

The acer in the garden at Spindlewood was probably planted when the house was built in the 60s and is now a mature and elegant tree. As the owner explained: "In the spring the leaves are bright reddish brown, then they go brown through the summer, only going bright red the week before they fall." From what I can tell this cultivar is either 'Bloodgood', 'Fireglow' or 'Ariandne', and there are hundreds of others.

Carl Peter Thunberg

Japanese maple is a native of Japan, Korea, China and eastern Mongolia. In the late C18th a Swedish doctor and botanist C P Thunberg travelling in Japan, produced drawings of a small tree with elegant leaves that would eventually become a favourite in oriental and western gardens. He gave the species the name 'palmatum' after the hand-like shape of the leaves (acer is Latin for 'sharp').

They have also been likened to frogs hands. We also see this shape (but much less pronounced) in the other maples and horse chestnut. And likewise this maple produces small winged seed samara, in this case at quite a pronounced angle of between 45 and 90 degrees. The flowers are produced in small cymes - multiple tiny flowers grouped on a stem - with five red or purple sepals and five whitish petals.

In Japanese culture the tree is highly regarded, and associated with grace, serenity and calm. I can certainly attest to that as I waited in its shade for a hazy sun to peer through the clouds. And even now the branches are bare, she has left a delicate carpet of crispy red leaves all around. So it might be that when it comes time for us to begin to shed our leaves we ought to do it gracefully.

(This tree is on private land - but you can see it from almost everywhere)

The glorious **Japanese maple** at Spindlewood near the church in late November, with a beautiful carpet underneath.

The leaves are said to resemble frogs fingers.

Juniper
(*Juniperus communis*)

Juniper trees in Sheepscombe? Yes there are, but you'll have to look very carefully, some of ours are still tiny and carefully shielded from harm. Natural England have a project to re-introduce Juniper up on the common, and two are growing under their protective 'cage' near to the entrance to Lord's Wood.

You'll need to get down low and peer through the wire, but they are well worth the effort, even though they are only four or five inches high. Juniper is very slow-growing and can take up seven years even to reach a height of 20 cm. While they are so small, they are vulnerable to being eaten by deer, rabbits, voles and sheep.

This is a rare and threatened coniferous native. It dates back 10,000 years and was one of the first to colonise the UK after the last ice age. Juniper is evergreen and has very tightly packed foliage of spiky needle-like leaves, arranged in threes on ridged twigs. Needles are distinctive with a single pale band on the upper surface and are grey-green beneath. If crushed, they smell of apples.

On Juniper Hill, south of Bull's Cross on the north slopes of the ridge, you will find several good-sized specimens, and quite a few seedlings under frames, protected from grazing on the steep sides of an abandoned quarry - a very similar habitat to our common. There are also some growing on Painswick Beacon.

The dense cover that juniper provides is ideal protection for nesting birds. This is a dioecious species - the male and female structures grow on separate trees. The male parts are small, yellow and spherical, and grow at the base of the needles near the twig tips. The female cones start green but darken to blue-black over 18 months and end up looking like blueberries - although they are not actually berries.

Juniper has always been a popular flavouring for gin. The first records of gin-making are from Salerno in southern Italy where Benedictine monks would distil fiery, alcoholic tonics made from wine infused with juniper berries. The word gin is itself derived from 'jenever', a Dutch/Belgian liquor, once a medicine.

The wood is aromatic, has a warm, golden colour and is suited to wood turning and carving as well as for burning to smoke food and as an incense. The berries produce an oil which can be used to aid respiratory and digestive problems and can be made into a tincture or in a tea, useful for aiding urinary complaints.

The diminutive but sturdy **juniper** under a frame on the Common by the entrance to Lord's Wood.

Established tree on Juniper Hill, about 1km along from Bull's Cross on the north side of the ridge.

Blue mature female cones, and yellow male cones.

Julie Wood

pedia

The juniper on Sheepscombe common were planted from berries - or more accurately cones as they are called - from Painswick Beacon, and are part of a two-fold long term project.

The first aim of the project is to re-establish juniper on some of the sites where it used to be found, there are old records for juniper on Sheepscombe Common. Juniper is highly flammable and it is likely that, as with many of the grassland commons, juniper disappeared from Sheepscombe when burning began to replace grazing in the early 20th century. The second aim of the project is to grow disease free plants that can eventually be used to increase the genetic diversity of the remaining junipers on Juniper Hill, all of which are either clones or descendants of just two plants.

Painswick Beacon has quite a number of juniper bushes so the obvious thing to do would be to sow seed from Painswick Beacon onto Juniper Hill to increase the diversity. However, juniper is susceptible to disease, in particular Phytophthora austrocedri, a pathogen that infects and kills junipers. There is absolutely no evidence of this disease in the Cotswolds and also no evidence that it can be transmitted via the seed. However, with so few junipers left on Juniper Hill, we are proceeding with extreme caution as nobody wants to be responsible for wiping out juniper from Juniper Hill! It is also an opportunity to bring back juniper to some of the commons, making the larger juniper population more secure in the event that something happened on Painswick Beacon.

Juniper supports more than 35 species of invertebrate, some of which are juniper specialists such as the juniper shield bug and juniper carpet moth, and the berries are eaten by many birds such as thrushes and fieldfares, so as well as its aesthetic and historical value, it is an important plant in its own right.

Kate Gamez - Natural England

At the height of The Plague in the C14[th], some doctors dressed in flowing black robes, their faces covered by masks with an elongated nose cone stuffed with juniper amongst other herbs. The purpose of the mask was to keep away bad smells - miasma - which were believed to be the principal cause of the disease. They thought it might counter the "evils" of the plague and prevent them from becoming infected.

So I guess we can be grateful for small mercies, as we can for tiny junipers.

Insets: New needle growth, young red female cone and yellow male cone.
Twig with mass of needles. Bark close-up.

Larch in winter
on Saltridge Hill

Larch

(Larix decidua)

If you're looking up at the branches of an untidy conifer, strangely bare of needles, with tight little cones still attached to knobbly twigs - then chances are you are in front of a larch in winter. And if larch is the Cinderella conifer in our winter woodlands, then she makes up for it in spring when new needles emerge and clothe her in little bright green bunches.

Up on Saltridge Hill where larch and Scots pine stand side by side it is almost impossible to tell them apart by bark alone. Both are fissured and scaly,

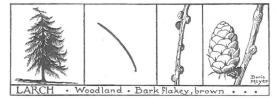

although in Scots pine a gradual redness shows higher up. The larch can grow to a lofty 45m.

Larch was introduced to Britain in the 17th century and planted in huge numbers in Scotland for the quality of its timber and the straightness of its trunk. In Dunkeld "The Parent Larch" is a 275 year old specimen, one of several brought over by the Duke of Atholl as seedlings from the Austrian Tyrol at the start of mass plantings in Scotland.

Being deciduous, larch plantations allow a fair amount of light down to the forest floor from autumn through to spring. This in turn allows some ground flora a chance to thrive. The common crossbill is a visitor, using its specialised beak to part the cone scales and reach the seed. Siskin and redwing are also fond of the seeds. Some moth caterpillars feed on the needles, including the casebearer and larch pug.

Larch cone (F Norman)

Along with spruce, pine and birch, larch has proved hardy enough to occupy the highest latitudes of any tree on earth - the taiga or boreal forests of Siberia, Scandinavia and Canada. You may also come across Japanese larch or a hybrid of this and the European variety[1] but these are hard to tell apart.

The cones of Japanese larch are more open than its European cousin, and looks rather like a woody rose-bud. The hybrid larch is visually somewhere between those of its parents but is more vigorous than either and sturdier in the face of harsh climates and poor soil.

Recently Scottish larch has been threatened by a fungus - Phytophthora ramorum (also known as Sudden Oak Death) which attacks both larch and oak. This is spread by airborne spores and is deadly, with no known cure. The only prevention is to fell infected trees to hopefully stop the fungus spreading. In recent years it has been discovered further south too.

Like Scots pine, larch is not good for firewood, being resinous it spits and can produce a sticky residue in your flue.

Untidy knobbly winter branches.

Both reproductive parts are found on the same tree. The female cones first show as crimson in the spring but then become brown and woody as they mature, standing out proud on the branch. They ripen and release their seeds in the first year, but stubbornly persist on the branch well into the next year. The male parts are soft yellow cones, releasing their pollen in the spring.

Larch is tough for a softwood, resistant to rot, and can withstand cycles of wet and dry without cracking or warping. It is widely used for gates, fencing (larch lap), garden furniture, posts and also in boat-building. You will find larch in amongst our beechwoods, as it is grows faster than beech, and began the regeneration of the canopy, encouraging the beech ever-upwards.

Being so prevalent in northern climes, it is perhaps not surprising that larch features in the folk-law of the of northern Siberia and Lapland. There, shamans have it as their "World Tree", symbolically connecting earth to heaven and the wood incorporated into their ceremonial drums.

On our high streets you can even find essence of larch for sale as one of the Bach Remedies, designed to promote self-confidence and assertiveness. Armed with such a potion, you *shall* go to the ball.

[1]Japanese larch (Larix kaempferi), hybrid larch (Larix x marchlinsii)

Lilac

(Syringa vulgaris)

Another one with heart-shaped leaves (to join mulberry, lime, hazel and catalpa), the lilac tree/bush is deciduous and part of the olive family - oleaceae. It has opposing buds and is well known and loved for its conical clusters (panicles) of small, very fragrant, 4-lobed tubular flowers that bloom in late spring or early summer.

Common lilac was introduced from the mountains of south-east Europe in the 1500s as a garden plant, and has since become naturalised. It is reasonably rare outside of gardens but can be found in hedgerows and along woodland edges and here in the field across the road from the village hall. The wood is hard, fine-grained and mainly used for turning small objects and for carving, but not used for furniture given the small size of the plant.

There are widespread stories that bringing white lilacs into the house was unlucky, possibly due to the old practice of using the flowers to mask the scent of death by placing them in a coffin. On a lighter note we enjoy the familiar smell in soap, perfume and cosmetics these days.

The RHS tells me that lilac is 'easy to grow in most well-drained, fertile, humus-rich alkaline to neutral soils. Thrives in chalky ground and appreciates mulching when planted in full sun. Dislikes strongly acidic soils'.

In some traditions Lilac is associated with playful flirtation (hearts again), and the blooming of new but maybe fleeting love. Indeed the lilac is only in full flower for a couple of weeks, so be careful who you dally with under those heady blooms!

(This tree is on private land - but you can see it from the road)

The **lilac** in the field across the road from the village hall.

Lime, common

(tilia x europaea)

As pilgrimages go, the trek from the village up the Sheepscombe valley to the Foston's Ash pub is neither arduous nor conventionally spiritual. Nonetheless, as travellers emerge from the gloom of the beechwoods into daylight on the Cotswold uplands they are greeted by a row of five majestic limes announcing that earthly refreshment is not far away.

Common lime is a hybrid of the large and the small-leaved lime, (tilia platyphyllos and tilia cordata) and are hard to tell apart save for the size of their leaves. They are easily identified in spring and summer by their serrated heart-shaped slightly lop-sided leaves. These are quite fragile and decay quickly once fallen, with the result that smaller plants are able to thrive underneath and not smothered as in a beech wood.

If you are keen to tell exactly which type of lime you have come across it is the underside of the leaf that is key. If it is hairy all over you have a large-leaved lime. If there are white hairs only along the leaf veins it is a common lime, and if rusty-red then you have a small-leaved lime.

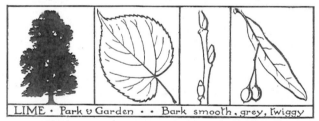

LIME · Park & Garden · · Bark smooth, grey, twiggy

Another clue is that large-leaved lime does not produce suckers from the base of the trunk as does its small cousin.

It's another tree popular with park and town planners due to being fast-growing, but try to avoid parking your car underneath as the sweet leaves are much-loved by aphids, and the resultant honey-dew rains down a sticky mess. These specimens were actually planted in memory of John Workman's mother who died in 1960.

Small-leafed lime leaves grow up to 8cm long, the large up to 15cm, and the common, somewhere between the two. On a hot day the large leaves can wilt, taking on a hooded appearance.

Lime tree row at the head of the Sheepscombe valley.

Limes are hermaphrodite - both male and female reproductive parts are contained within each flower - and these are greeny-yellow with five petals, hanging in clusters of between four and ten below a wing.

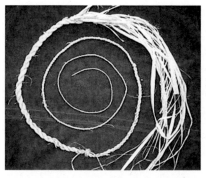

Lime bark cordage - naturallore blog

In late summer and though into winter you'll see the conspicuous small hard fruits hanging down on stalks under this single helicopter wing - used to aid dispersal like sycamore and field maple. The bark is pale grey-brown and smooth when young, becoming irregularly fissured with age.

Cut lime wood is soft and light, white-yellow in appearance and finely textured. It is easy to work with and often used in turnery, carving and furniture making. Lime bark was traditionally used to make rope, and lime flowers were considered a valuable source of food for bees (look out for lime honey).

Lime wood resists warping and is still used today to make sounding boards and piano keys. Limes, especially the small-leaved variety, can be coppiced and used for fuel, hop-poles, bean-sticks, cups, ladles, bowls and even Morris dancing sticks. During the privations of war-time, lime blossom was used to make a soothing tea.

Symbolically lime (linden) trees used to be be planted in rows, most often In France and Switzerland, as a symbol of liberty, and to celebrate success in battles.

If you don't want to go quite so far as the head of our valley to find lime, there's a fine specimen in the grounds of The Grange in the middle of the village, easily viewed from the road.

There is a lime tree at Westonbirt Arboretum that is now a ring of coppiced growths and is said to be 2000 years old. So who knows, maybe a pilgrimage is in order.

London plane
(and lad with football) enjoying the autumn sunshine in the field below the Far End post box.

94

London Plane
(Planatus x Hispanica)

The city comes to Sheepscombe! This tree makes a statement wherever it grows and is clearly enjoying being in our sleepy valley, but it does seem rather out of place. It's rarely seen 'in the wild' so my guess is that our example was deliberately planted.

You are much more likely to find this plane lining our capital's streets and parks. It accounts for more than half of London's tree population and there are plenty in Cheltenham and Gloucester too, as it is widely favoured by town planners due to its tolerance of pollution and stately bearing.

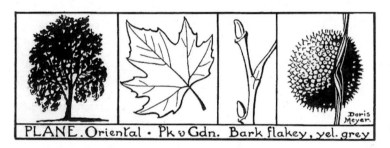

PLANE. Oriental • Pk v Gdn. Bark flakey, yel. grey

You'd be forgiven for confusing London plane with sycamore or maple initially, but plane has much larger palmate leaves - which can be more than twice the size of an adult hand, flaky, scaly bark and those tell-tale spiky fruits dangling down.

The tree is monoecious, so both male and female ball-shaped flowers are found on the same specimen, although on different stems. It is a deciduous hardwood species often growing to 30m or more.

After pollination by wind, the female flowers develop into spiky fruits, comprising a dense cluster of seeds with stiff hairs, which aid dispersal by the wind. The fruits slowly break up over winter to release their seeds.

Plane is not a native of our shores and its lineage is unclear, but most likely it is a hybrid between the American sycamore and Oriental plane that appeared in the UK in the early 17th century.

It first found itself planted en masse on London's streets around the time of the Industrial Revolution when the air was thick with soot and smoke.

London plane sheds its bark in flakes regularly - a useful defence in a polluted environment - and the huge smooth leaves readily wash clean in a shower.

Freshly cut timber shows an unusual colouration of pinks and peaches, which turn a creamy brown as it dries.

It is a strong hardwood with similar properties to oak and has a dense attractive grain. It's not that durable outside but does make excellent furniture and is used in turning and carving.

When quarter-sawn[1] into planks or made into veneer, the wood can show an unusual speckled or lace-like effect from the way the trunk's medullary rays[2] are revealed and this gives rise to the description 'lacewood'.

Despite its pollution-defying attributes, those huge leaves do cause a problem on our streets in autumn, covering pavements in a slippery mush, blocking drains and blighting the lives of street sweepers.

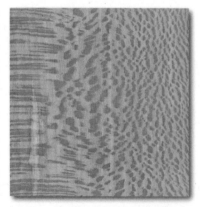

Lacewood veneer pattern in plane (photo: wood-database.com)

Rail travellers are not immune either, as these are no doubt some of the 'wrong type of leaves' on the line.

[1] The log is first cut radially into quarters and then sawn diagonally as if towards the centre.
[2] Sheets or ribbons of cells that run from the inside to the outside of the trunk.

Monkey Puzzle
(*Araucaria araucana*)

Central to the stream-side garden at Brooklands, below the school, is a spiky giant that towers above most of its companions. In my youth, a neighbour's 'monkey puzzle' was the nearest I got to exotic lands and invoked images of confused simians sitting around scratching their heads.

This is a fine specimen, around 20m tall, with a dead-straight trunk of considerable girth. The owner estimated it could be close to 120 years old as

it is a similar size to some at Westonbirt with that age. It is native to South America, and is the national tree of Chile, where it is called Pehuén by the Pehuenche people who use the seeds as part of their staple diet.

Also known as Chilean pine (though not a true pine), it is another ancient (and we have a few in Sheepscombe) known to have existed around 200 million years ago and is said to live for up to 1000 years. Its large and tasty seeds,

The nuts: Intact, with inner skin and peeled. (rawedibleplants.blogspot)

called piñones, take two years to mature. They are perfectly edible and can be made into a pesto having a taste similar to pine nuts.

Small male cones and the larger female cones usually develop on different trees. The seeds are not winged and like other conifers the tree relies on birds or rodents for seed dispersal.

For this tree it is pigeons and corvids that nest in the lofty branches and no doubt diet on the inaccessible nuts.

The charming common name seems to have become popular from the mid-1800s when a Cornish gardener was proudly showing off his rare

The impressive **monkey puzzle** at Brooklands.

specimen to visitors and one noted individual was heard to say "It would puzzle a monkey to climb that!". So the name 'monkey puzzler' and later 'monkey puzzle' stuck.

It is certainly a hardy individual, not only evident by its longevity, but its thick trunk is said to give some resistance to forest fires and even volcanic ash. One of its native habitats is in volcanic soil with obvious attendant hazards.

The wood is little used these days as the tree is on the endangered list due to logging. It does however produce a tight straight-grained softwood that used to be popular for small turned and speciality items as it is quite easy to work.

Leaves & mature cone (H Zell - Wiki)

The only puzzle remaining is how this one got here, by whom and when - does anyone know?

In its natural habitat in the Conguillío National Park in the Chilean Andes with the Lliama volcano. (P Hurtado - Pixabay)

(This tree is on private land - but it is visible from the path)

greenandvibrant.com

The **black mulberry** across from the pub.

Black Mulberry

(Morus nigra)

And so it was, the other week, sitting in the sun outside The Butcher's with my pie and my pint - what's that leaning over the wall where everyone parks, with big heart-shaped leaves?

A little autumn-ragged now, this one is growing against the wall at Farundell in what used to be the kitchen garden of the Old Vicarage.

This is the black mulberry variant which were imported in to the UK in the 17th century in the mistaken belief that silkworms would feed on the leaves - they didn't - they preferred white mulberry 'morus alba', whose leaves are oval rather than heart-shaped. Nonetheless the trees proved popular in country-house gardens as they grew spreading and gnarly and full of character.

This is a small but broad and shady, deciduous tree whose characteristic leaves are downy on the underside, but with short spiky hairs on the top. Flowers form on spikes - the males are green and larger than the lighter female flowers.

The fruits are tasty and start out looking just like raspberries before turning dark when ripe - but watch out, they will stain fingers and clothes! The leaves can suffer from a bacterial spot-growth which can cause dieback. Bark is orange-brown and the trunks often fissured and twisted.

In literature and legend, mulberry has an interesting place: It appears in the works of Ovid and in Shakespeare's "A Midsummer Night's Dream" in the tale of Pyramus and Thisbe.

These ill-fated lovers were forbidden to wed, and so arranged to meet secretly under a mulberry tree. Due to a combination of tragic mistake and grief (as so often), they both ended up dead under the tree. In response, and no doubt to honour the fact that these two lovers were faithful to the end, the gods decided to stain the mulberry's white fruits dark red.

Sericulture is the process of silk production from moth-eggs through to strands of the finest thread. The female silk-moth 'Bombyx mori' lays hundreds of eggs, which are kept incubated until they hatch into larvae. These caterpillars are fed on a diet of white mulberry leaves for about 6 weeks until they stop feeding.

At this point the silkworm begins to build its cocoon by gyrating its body in a figure-of-eight pattern hundreds of thousands of times, while producing the thread from holes in its mouth, along with a gum that binds it all together. By the time it has finished - around 72 hours later - this industrious creature has produced around 100m of thread, and has cocooned itself ready to pupate.

Unfortunately for the silkworm the cocoons are then dropped into boiling water to dissolve the gum and allow the silk to be extracted and wound onto a reel. It takes around 2,500 silkworms to produce around 500g of silk.

(Biddle Sawyer Silks)

And the origins of "here we go round the mulberry bush"? This children's rhyme, usually taken to mean 'oh no, here we go again', has been said to have originated in Wakefield women's prison in the mid 1800s where such a specimen grew in the middle of the exercise yard.

Mind you, with a bit of cunning and a few thousand silkworms, surely the inmates could at least have spun a rope-ladder?

(This tree is on private land - but it is visible from the road)

English Oak

(Quercus robur)

Three very different fates awaited you if were a British oak in the 16th to 18th century. If you grew straight and true, you were felled for shipwrights and palace builders. But if you were more haphazard in your growth, you might be coppiced or be clambered upon by eager children.

Here in the village you will have no doubt seen that we have two types - the traditional mighty upright resident as on the village green, and several examples of the climbing types on the common below the cricket pitch. Oaks that grow in the open with no competition tend to be the sprawling ones and ours may have got to be the way they are by human lopping or cattle browsing them in their formative years. For the British surely no tree is more majestic,

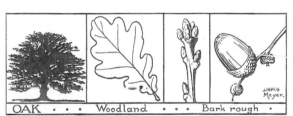

OAK · · · Woodland · · · Bark rough ·

solid, dependable or doughty than the oak.

Quercus robur is known as 'pendunculate' due to its acorns being on long stalks. I haven't spotted if we have any of the other less common form 'sessile' (quercus petraea) with acorns that grow directly off the twig with no stalk. The sessile oak is more common in the west of the British Isles, in hilly areas and is the national tree of Ireland. There are plenty of other species in the UK, including downy, red, turkey, cork and holm (see box).

In the past, the Forest of Dean and the New Forest amongst others, were major suppliers of oak timber for such ships as the Mary Rose and those later used against the Armada. It is said that a major fighting ship could consume as many as 600 trees. In the New Forest, 'inclosures' were fenced areas protecting valuable oak stock against grazing and damaging by cattle.

So vital was this supply, that in 1698 an Act of Parliament outlawed the coppicing of oak (common for firewood and fence posts), and particularly valuable trees would be given the King's Mark, denoting property of the Crown. The roof beams of Westminster Abbey are of durmast timber from sessile oaks.

The King's mark.

Village green **English oak** and close up of its blighted leaves, possibly rust fungus. **Holm oak** leaves. In the climbing oak on the common. Pendunculate leaves and acorns. (c/w from above)

The English oak is a long-lived deciduous tree, growing 20 to 40m tall, with often a massive fissured trunk and sturdy branches culminating in a dense crown. Leaves are almost unmistakable, deeply lobed and on very short stalks. Acorns are not produced until the tree is around 30 or 40 years old. Its peak fecundity is around 80 - 100 years, after which growth slows but the tree can live for several hundred years. The canopy allows a fair amount of light down to the forest floor, and this promotes diversity of plant and animal life below.

Holm oak. One of the few evergreen broadleaf trees, holm oak is most easily spotted in winter, when most around is bare. Leaves are ovate with a pointed tip and round base, dark and shiny above, but downy on the underside, and when young are spiny a little like holly leaves. Its Latin name of Quercus Ilex and common name 'holly oak' reflect this likeness. After pollination, female flowers develop into acorns. These are smaller than the English oak and have a more pointed tip.

It's a native to the Eastern Mediterranean but has been naturalised in the UK, having been brought over in the 1500s. They are known to be resistant to salt spray so have been used as wind-breaks on the coast. They're not that tolerant of freezing conditions however, so I hope ours In the village survive our current sub-zero spell in the valley (December 22).

Male and female catkins are produced in the spring along with the first flush of leaves, which are often eaten by insects and so a 'Lammas' second growth of leaves can occur midsummer.

When acorns turn brown and fall in autumn they provide a rich food source for jays, mice and squirrels and historically were fed to pigs and cattle. Oak has always been a favourite for furniture, doors and gates with its beautiful dense grain. The process of tanning leather has traditionally relied on the tannin from oak bark to process and preserve.

The oldest oaks, standing alone, and those at the top of a hill, often show the dreadful scars of one or more lightning strikes, and perhaps it's not surprising that the tree is sacred to Zeus, Jupiter, Dagda and Thor (Greek, Roman, Celtic and Teutonic gods).

So if you are out on the hill in stormy weather, choose your trees and your gods with care.

The **common pear** in the field across the stream from Flock Mill - but mind the cattle!

Common Pear

(Pyrus communis)

Assuming you aren't phased by the herd of adolescent cattle that are often stomping around in the field, you might be interested in crossing the stream just below Flock Mill and striding up the other side. You'll pass some interesting characters - alder, poplar, tulip tree, and a little further up a pear tree. What's so unusual about that, I hear you ask, aren't there are quite a few fruit tree escapees around the valley?

But this one is huge. Standing probably a full 20m tall, it looks like it's never been pruned or harvested, but simply left to its own devices. We were pretty astonished at first meeting and stayed under its dappled shade for quite a while (with half an eye on the row of inquisitive heads watching us).

Also known as the European pear, originating from western Asia, the tree has been cultivated for its fruit for millennia and is thought to have originally been a hybrid of the Wild and Caucasian (Pyrus pyraster and Pyrus caucasica) species.

Characterised by its cracked and squared bark, oval leaves with tiny serrations and five-petal white flowers - these were just over on the late spring day we were there. The fruit of the cultivars are our typical pear shape, soft and juicy, whereas those from the wild species are smaller and rounder. Pear is one of the Rosaceae family - along with other orchard fruit trees and hawthorn, rowan, raspberry, strawberry and roses amongst others.

Pear wood is a very dense, fine-grained hardwood and and good for turning. It is prized for high-end furniture-making and in the production of some musical instruments. This is a relatively expensive wood, as pear trees are slow-growing and don't normally reach great heights. Moreover they are most often grown for their fruit and so the wood can't be harvested until the tree has stopped producing, and this can take decades. Even during seasoning, time and care is needed, as the wood can twist during drying and so must be placed under a lot of pressure during this process

As a firewood it burns well with a sweet aroma - good for smoking meats - but it needs to be well-seasoned as it is so dense it takes a long time to dry out.

Another benefit of its hard consistency is pear wood's ability to hold up to heat and moisture, and to be carved into intricate designs that would be impossible in softer woods.

The art of wood-cut printing makes use of this quality of as it allows very fine carving which then holds its edge well over many printings.

In Greek mythology, pears are sacred to the goddesses Hera and Aphrodite. In ancient Chinese folk-law it was believed that the pear was a symbol of immortality, but also of separation.

This possibly due to the fact that a pear is womb-shaped, indicating not only life but the child eventually separating from the mother. Thus some think it unlucky to share a pear between two people.

On a lighter note, pear-based alcoholic drinks are popular of course: perry is a pear-based cider, and there are several pear schnapps' and brandies available.

Pear wood gingerbread mould by György Kövér (Etsy)

Which leads me to wonder: if no-one collects the fallen fruits from this pear tree in our valley - would our friends the adolescent beef cattle, gorge on them and then become loud and unruly? I think we should be told.

Black poplar
(*Populus nigra 'betulifolia'*)

Tall, broad and flexible, our native black poplar is most at home near water, or in boggy ground and in its slender Lombardy 'italica' cultivar, can often to be seen in rows along riverbanks. This one seems to be part-way between black and Lombardy and could be 'betulifolia', being a cross between the two. There are white and grey poplars too, and their leaves are nearer to the shape of aspen's but with slight lobing. Grey poplar is a hybrid of white and aspen.

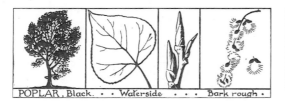

POPLAR, Black. · · Waterside · · · Bark rough ·

POPLAR, White

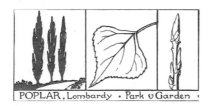

POPLAR, Lombardy · Park v Garden ·

Fluffy cotton wool seeds.

Black poplar's leaves are its biggest giveaway, as they are essentially a stylish triangle-shape with a fine-toothed edge. The tree's catkins look like big hairy caterpillars, and once pollinated, the females produce prodigious amounts of downy-white seeds looking like cotton wool, that can almost carpet the ground in late summer. Poplar is dioecious, meaning that male and female flowers are found on separate trees. They are a part of the saliceae family, along with the willows and aspen.

This is a fast-growing tree and in common with others like silver birch, is a soft hardwood, not that dense and prone to splitting - so it tends to get used for pallets, crates, upholstered furniture frames and paper. On a more positive note, poplar is buoyant and is used to make paddles and oars. It's too lightweight for fire logs but does make good kindling.

The imposing **black poplar** in the field below the school, near the valley footpath.

According to the Forestry Commission, black poplar is one of the most endangered native timber trees in Britain. There are concerns that there are so few black poplars in the countryside that it is unlikely they will pollinate each other. The poplar species is prone to a number of fungal diseases including leaf rusts, cankers and poplar scab.

In symbolism, poplar's location, tall stature and necessarily deep roots give rise to attributes of grounding, flexibility and an affinity with water and the wind. Also said to be known as the shield-makers tree since the wood was thought to offer protection from injury or death. In mythology, some sources have it that when Heracles returned from the underworld he was crowned with poplar leaves as this was a tree sacred to Hades.

It has been known from ancient times that chewing on the bark or leaves of willow or poplar could help with aches, pains and headaches, and from the early 1800s salicylic acid was extracted and is now produced synthetically as Aspirin.

^ *The Heliades were seven nymph daughters of the sun-god Helios. When their brother Phaethon was struck from the chariot of the sun by Zeus, they gathered around his smoky grave on the banks of the River Eridanos and in their unrelenting grief were transformed into poplar-trees and their tears into golden amber.*

(greekmythology.wikia.org)

In these uncertain times it is surely not a bad thing to be grounded, flexible and to be able to bend gracefully with the winds of change?

(This tree is on private land - but it is visible from the path)

111

From top: male and female flowers and needles.
(flower pictures - A Peace treeblog.co.uk)

Scots pines up on Saltridge Hill.

Scots Pine

(Pinus sylvestris)

Dark and mysterious. Roamed by bears, wolves, lynx and wild boar, the Caledonian Forest once covered much of the Scottish Highlands. Scots pines dominated, and were the first pines to arrive on our shores after the Late Glacial period (c8000 BC). There are still some remnants of that ancient forest left north of the border although sadly they are less red in tooth and claw.

Most of our own pines can be found up on Saltridge Hill, overlooking the confluence of the Cranham and Sheepscombe valleys and these are a deliberate planting. It's a wise choice of tree for the position - Scots pine is strong and hardy, and with a long tap root is well suited to this exposed location. In these woods you will also find they are mixed with larch and that beech has moved in too. Down in the village there are a few examples to be found, notably those on the way down from the pub to the village hall.

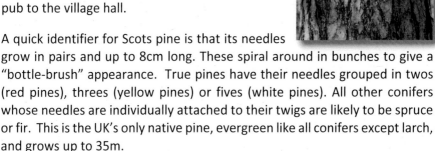

A quick identifier for Scots pine is that its needles grow in pairs and up to 8cm long. These spiral around in bunches to give a "bottle-brush" appearance. True pines have their needles grouped in twos (red pines), threes (yellow pines) or fives (white pines). All other conifers whose needles are individually attached to their twigs are likely to be spruce or fir. This is the UK's only native pine, evergreen like all conifers except larch, and grows up to 35m.

Young bark is a scaly copper-red but darkens and fissures further with age. Also, as it grows, lower branches fall away - they don't get much light anyway - and the tree concentrates its energies to branching and flowering higher up in the canopy of the forest.

In Scotland it is a unique habitat that supports the capercaille, crested tit and crossbill - the latter's adapted beak is able to extract the seeds from the cones. red squirrel and pine marten are also dependant on the Caledonian Forest.

Our southern pine forests are mainly planted for timber and are home to long-eared and tawny owls, woodpeckers, treecreepers and goldcrests.

At ground level pine forests can appear barren and lifeless. There is little green growth due to the smothering layers of pine needles, and on Saltridge, beech leaves too. But mosses, fungi and ferns do thrive, especially on stumps and fallen trees, and these also provide a home for bugs and beetles. Ants make their home under the needle-floor especially if the soil is sandy. You will also

PINE, Scots. • Woodland • Bark flakey, reddish orange

find the occasional holly and yew which don't mind the dull conditions.

Scots pine is monoecious - both male and female flowers grow on the same tree. Male flowers are yellow and upright, while the female flower is small, red and bud-like, growing at the tips of new shoots. After pollination, the females turn green and develop into cones. These don't mature until the following season, so those familiar cones are two years old when they open.

The tree produces a durable softwood, popular for furniture, and is one of the woods chosen for utility poles and once used for pit props. It is called deal when sawn, to make gates and doors, and in the production of chipboard and paper pulp.

Trunks destined to be telephone or electricity poles are de-barked and seasoned in the open air for up to 18 months. Poles tend to be about 9 m long (including 2 m in the ground) and 150 to 200 mm in diameter. Once seasoned they are pressure-treated with creosote or the more benign copper biocide depending on the final usage. Treated poles can be placed directly in the ground and can last for more than 30 years.

The Celts saw pine as a tree of protection and strength and burnt the needles to disperse negative energy or sickness. As an infusion it has an antiseptic action or hot and steaming is a decongestant for respiratory disorders. Some burn the resin for incense. Although it makes good charcoal, don't put pine wood on the fire as it spits and over time resinous deposits from the smoke can choke up chimneys.

With plans afoot to reintroduce wolves to Scottish forests, maybe we should follow suit down here. It would certainly make picnics more exciting.

Spindle
(Euonymus europaea)

"I coulde never learne an Englishe name for it. The Duche men call it in Netherlande, 'spilboome', that is, spindel-tree, because they use to make spindels of it in that country, and me thynke it may be as well named in English seying we have no other name." – 16th century botanist William Turner.

Delicate yet strong, colourful and practical, beautiful but poisonous, spindle is a slender, spreading bush/tree, and spends most of the year living

incognito in our hedges and forest-edges. But come autumn, its pale green flowers become bright pink/orange fruits and the leaves turn red-orange and they are easy to spot.

The fruits hang on long after the leaves have fallen. Leaves are oval with a pointed end and tiny serrations around the edge. They are short-stemmed and grow in opposition along the stem.

This example has been boxed in by fencing, which puzzled me until I realised that it was poisonous to sheep and cattle if eaten in quantity.

I can't think of another species that is so clearly named after its major historical use. The wood is dense and grows straight-grained by-and-large and was used for everything from tooth-picks to knitting needles to cattle-prods as well as spindles used in wool-spinning.

Spindle stem

Spindle's usefulness doesn't stop there: as a dense wood it makes strong charcoal pencils for artists, and the berries used to be used as a laxative and as a cure for head-lice in humans and mange in cattle.

Late autumn **spindle** in the field opposite Coldstream Cottages.

Buds develop in an opposite pattern and the flowers are hermaphrodite - containing both male and female components. However they generally still need pollinating from other specimens, usually by insects.

Wildlife find this tree equally beneficial. The flowers produce a lot of nectar which attracts a variety of insects such as hover-flies, bees and aphids. The magpie moth and scorched-carpet moth are visitors, as are the spindle ermine and holly blue butterflies. The caterpillar of the spindle ermine can be a pest as it munches on the leaves.

These insects do of course provide a ready food source for many birds such as Robins, Blue Tits and Great Tits. It is said that in some parts of the country the tree was once called 'Robin's Bread' and they seem to be the main distributor of the seeds.

< The Spinner' by W-A Bouguereau, shows a woman hand-spinning using a drop spindle. The fibres to be spun are on a distaff spindle held in her left hand.

(picture Wikipedia)

Threats to spindle are mainly the spider mite, vine weevil and sap-feeding scale insect which which can cause dieback.

If I remember correctly Sleeping Beauty's coma was supposedly brought on by pricking her finger on the spindle she was using. Could it have been that the 'wicked witch' used a concoction from the berries and leaves smeared on the tip to do the evil deed? Oh the perils of youth! Mind you, it ended well.

(This tree is on private land - but it is visible from the road)

The venerable **sweet chestnut** at Dell Farm. About 30m high, 6m girth and over 200 years old.

Sweet Chestnut
(Castanea sativa)

You won't be going barefoot under sweet chestnut in autumn. Beneath the few we have in Sheepscombe, the ground is littered with the prickly nut cases, split open - a ready feast for squirrels and mice. Other identifiers for this tree are the long, toothed leaves and bark that is ridged and often spirals upwards.

It is a sturdy and characterful tree, related to the oak, and is similarly capable of great height, girth and longevity. This venerable character grows on Dell

Farm, below Longridge. Over the years the owner's daughter and friends have delighted in climbing up its gnarled and generous trunk. It is thought to be over 200 years old.

A versatile tree for us humans, it is widely coppiced, and is used for turning, for making into fence poles and for charcoal.

The leaves were once gathered to make bedding for the poor, who called them "talking beds" after the rustling produced when lain on. These are the nuts that are typically sold roasted on the streets of our big cities in winter.

The eye of the Dell Farm tree - a useful foothold on the way up.

Due to its high density, it burns hot and slow in the fireplace, but is prone to splitting. Some wine casks are made of the wood which performs well in the wet, being full of tannins.

This is a deciduous, non-native species, believed to have been brought over by the Romans early in their occupation, and the nuts made into porridge or ground to flour to feed their army. Unlike other nuts, sweet chestnuts are rich in carbohydrate rather than protein, and have historically been cooked and eaten in times of hardship.

Don't confuse this with horse chestnut, whose nuts are inedible, with cases that are much less spiky, and with compound leaves (made up of leaflets), rather than a single leaf.

Long yellow male catkins are produced in the spring, along with a few green females, clustered at the base. This makes the tree monoecious having both male and female parts on the same tree. The tree prefers a light, well-drained soil and you won't see nuts develop until it is about 25 years old.

Long yellow catkins (photo: Maja Dumat)

There's not a lot of folklore associated with sweet chestnut, probably because it's not a native, but historically it has been used to make tea, and is said to help with respiratory conditions.

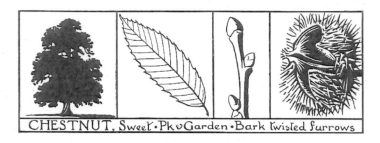

CHESTNUT, Sweet·Pk∨Garden·Bark twisted furrows

The nuts on sale in this country are likely from Southern Europe, but if you want to try a few you have found locally, here is an untested method of oven roasting:

Pre-heat to 400 F, 200 C, Gas Mark 6. Pare each one with an 'X' to allow the steam to escape and prevent exploding. Roast until the skin begins to open up and peel back to show they are ready – the 'X' then aids peeling the shell off.

Recipe from: blog.italian-pewter.co.uk

Far from home in his draughty barracks on Hadrian's Wall, a Roman legionary finishes his warming chestnut porridge and honey, sighs, pushes back his stool and steps out into the snow of a harsh northern winter.

(This tree is on private land)

Sycamore

(Acer pseudoplatanus)

Sycamore young don't fall very far from the tree, and in spring you'll often see a carpet of tiny saplings sprouting up near the parents. Some Foresters consider them weeds, so prolific is sycamore in propagating itself.

It's quite common in our woods and can be readily identified, winter or summer. A member of the maple family (with field and Norway maple and London plane) it has similar-shaped palmate leaves, much larger than 'field', but smaller than 'London'. The leaves are often blighted by 'tar spot' - a fungal growth which actually doesn't seem to harm the tree. Like all maples, sycamore shows symmetrical bud growth. Its winged seeds or 'samaras' grow in pairs at right angles, unlike field maple whose seeds

SYCAMORE · Pk & Gdn · Bark smooth, grey, flakey

are set at around 180 deg. The bark starts smooth but gets patchy and flaky with age. Possibly brought over by the Romans, sycamore later found favour as a park and garden tree, but then made good its escape into woodlands.

C17th horticulturalist John Evelyn wasn't impressed with the tree, and wrote in his seminal work *Sylva* in 1664: "The Sycomor . . . is much more in reputation for its shade than it deserves: for the Honey-dew leaves, which fall early turn to Mucilage . . . and putrefie with the first moisture of the season; so as they contaminate and marr our walks . . ." The honey-dew that annoyed Evelyn so much is the secretions of aphids that will drip onto unwary cars below.

It is 1834 and six men would meet regularly under the village green sycamore in the village of Tolpuddle in Dorset. They were all agricultural labourers, struggling to provide for their families under decreasing wages and dire living conditions. They formed what was essentially an early trade union to protest, but were shipped off to penal colonies in Australia for their pains. The subsequent outcry at home resulted in a mass march through London of some 100,000 people. As a result the men were brought home and pardoned. The 'Martyrs' Tree' still stands in memory of their struggle. And quite right too.

Mucilage. Such a great word. Remind me to use it more often.

(These trees are on private land - but are visible from the road/track)

The grand old **sycamore** up behind Greycot on Far End Lane, possibly 150 years old, its trunk and a leaf showing 'tar spot'.

Three musketeers of pollarded sycamore at the corner of the Ebworth Estate by Lord's Wood, where one of the estate entrances used to be.

Tulip Tree

(*Liriodendron tulipifera*)

The field below the Far End post box is home to quite a few leafy characters: London plane, walnut, fern-leaf beech as well as the regulars. But if you continue down and cross the stream under the row of alders, just downstream from Flock Mill, there is an another interesting individual to be found on the other side - just watch out for the cattle in the field.

There on the field-edge to the right is an elegant and exuberant tree - and in season you'll immediately spot its unique four-pointed leaves. Fast-growing, tall, with quivering leaves like poplar it is sometimes called tulip poplar - but is actually a relative of the magnolia. Like magnolia this has large leaves and opulent tulip-shaped flowers.

Flowers bloom in early summer, are 3–10 cm across and have three green outer sepals and six inner petals which are yellow-green with an orange flare at the base. The tree only starts flowering when semi-mature at around 15 to 20 years. In autumn, the leaves turn a delightful mixture of yellows and coppery-browns.

This one likes a moist but well-drained soil which is probably why it's down in the valley floor near to the stream, but not so close that its roots sit right in the water as alder likes to do.

Tulip tree wood is classed as a soft hardwood, with fine and straight grain which is easy to work. Typically used in cabinet and furniture-making where a cheap hardwood is wanted. As a firewood it is rather too light to give off much heat. The original peoples of North America - where this is a native species - called it 'canoewood', because its long fine grain and large trunks were well-suited for that purpose.

Medicinally it is not much used these days, but indigenous Americans and colonists reputedly would make a poultice from the leaves to treat inflammation and sores, made tea from the inner bark for fever and upset stomach, and use the root bark and seeds as a wormer.

So even if you're not troubled with an ague, I heartily recommend you meet this tree - it has the friendliest leaves in the valley.

The **tulip tree** near Flock Mill, across the Sheepscombe stream.

Below: the happiest leaves in the valley?

Kenpei - Wiki

Walnut

(*Juglans regia*)

Highly prized and with a racy name, what we know as English walnut was probably brought over here by the invading Romans who ground it into a nutty flour or squeezed it to a luxurious oil. Only later in the 18th century did we begin to use it in high end furniture-making.

It's a broadleaf deciduous tree, capable of growing up to 35m, and typically has a short trunk and broad crown, unless it happens to be in a woodland where it may grow a longer trunk in the competition for light. Young bark is smooth and olive-brown, but it develops fissures with age and also become more silver-grey.

Leaves are 'pinnate' - meaning feather-like with 5 to 9 oval leaflets each up to 15cm long, including a 'terminal' leaflet at the end. Crushed, they can smell like polish. The other variety you may come across is black walnut (Juglans nigra), whose distinguishing features are a darker bark, brighter leaves, but most obviously showing more like twice the number of leaflets which are also slimmer and more pointed. Leaves can show a black spotty blight, which can lead to dieback of new shoots and damaged fruit.

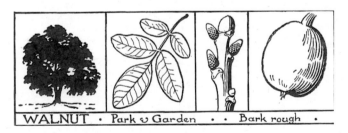

WALNUT · Park & Garden · · Bark rough ·

The male catkins are yellow, up to 15cm long, whilst the female flowers are small and greenish with yellow protruding stigma. The fruits in season are rounded and green, up to 5cm long encasing the tough walnut shell and its familiar contents.

Walnut is native in a wide band from south-east Europe to Asia. Said to have originated in Persia it may well have been traded along the Silk Road originally. Now widely planted in the UK it has naturalised in lowland Britain, probably assisted by diligent squirrels or mice.

The **walnut** in the field above Flock Mill, the trunk from one just along from Woody's Cottage and the fruit and leaves from Lord's Wood Cottage.

> **Fine cabinetry.** Since the Renaissance, both English and black walnut have been used in the construction of the most sought-after furniture both in the construction and as a veneer, due to its durability and extraordinarily beautiful grain in shades of brown and red. In 1709 a severe winter ruined much of the stock in central Europe and it became so scarce in France that an embargo was introduced banning the export or use of walnut until 1720. To make up for this loss in supplies, the British started to import from its colony in America the darker Virginia walnut.
>
> (Lapada guide to walnut in early 18th century furniture making - M Haughey)

Herbalists utilize various parts of walnut: Dried leaves of 'regia' can be used for the topical relief of inflammatory skin conditions such as eczema, psoriasis and to reduce excessive sweating of the hands and feet. The husk, shell and peel of 'nigra' are sudorific - sweat inducing - especially if used green.

Nutritionally, walnut kernels are a good source of antioxdants - substances that can can prevent or delay cellular damage caused by unstable molecules called free radicals. For example they contain proanthocyanidins, which may protect against sun damage, improve vision and increase blood circulation.

When I came upon this walnut for the first time I was dismayed to find that it was slowly being throttled by the wire netting originally put up presumably to protect it from deer and rabbit.

Returning the next day with wire cutters, we were pleased to be able to snip a line all the way up without damaging the bark. I swear I felt it heave a sigh of relief as the strictures fell away. And yes, we did hug it afterwards.

And the racy name? Roman mythology has it that their god Jupiter, or Jove had a fondness for walnuts while he walked upon the earth. So much so, that the Romans took to calling them 'Jovis glans' after part of his reproductive system. Which I imagine pleases him still.

The **wayfaring tree**/bush trying to keep a low profile. Sturdy stems with thick, symmetrical, serrated leaves and red berries.

Julie Wood

Julie Wood

Wayfaring Tree
(*Viburnum lantana*)

I've always been intrigued by this tree, and seeing as how I'd never spotted one until the other day, I had imagined this was an elusive character living up to his name. Rarely staying long in one place - keeping low perhaps, then upping sticks and wandering off down the track before dawn. But then, to our surprise, during an evening walk, there he was, tucked into a hedge on the lower edge of the Common, along on the left from the top of the track up from the pub.

Preferring chalk and limestone downlands, wayfarer is often more of a bush than a tree, growing untidily with multiple stems. Leaves are oval, toothed and thick with a layer of hairs on the underside. They grow in a determined symmetrical pattern, on sturdy stems, topped off with erect clusters of creamy white flowers. These give way in the late summer to bright red berries that then go to a dark purple as they ripen, becoming a feast for thrushes and warblers. Leaves turn orange and gold in the autumn.

From the viburnum family like Guelder rose - there are a number of similarities except for leaf shape and the fact that rose's flowers are different sizes whereas our wayfarer's are all the same size.

There is some debate as to how the name originated, but most writers suggest that it was once common along our hedgerows, tracks and field-edges, perhaps prompting C16th botanist John Gerard to have said "it is ever on the road". One hopes that actual wayfarers resting on a sunny bank didn't pick the berries, as they are an emetic.

Its young flexible branches seem to have once been in demand for binding up sheaves and bundles, an attribute given away by an old Wiltshire name 'hoar withy', the first part referring to the thick leaves, while 'withy' is an old word for willow. The wood of older stems is dense and straight and was once used to make arrow shafts - the Neolithic man found in an Austrian glacier in 1991 was carrying arrows made of viburnum wood.

Maybe this one didn't hear us coming, or maybe he'd just found the perfect spot to stop for a while. Anyway, if I were you I'd get up there soonish to look for him (or her) before they set off again.

Whitebeam on the common. Right: leaves and berries.
Left: **rowan** and **bastard service.** Centre: **Arran whitebeam**.

Whitebeam

(Sorbus aria)

With some trees, it pays to look down rather than up. Especially in winter, some are best identified by their leaf-scatter. Whitebeam and beech are two such, and leave us clues long into the next season, as their leaves are so slow to decay. Whitebeam identification is also helped by having leaves that are much paler on the underside and exhibit strong veining. There are several dotted around the common, the quarries and on the track above St George's Field. They do seem to like our rocky limestone soil.

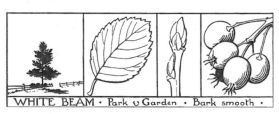

WHITE BEAM · Park & Garden · Bark smooth ·

A UK native and member of the Rosacea family, related to rowan and wild service, this is a compact and domed tree growing to a maximum of 15m. In spring she gives us clusters of 5-petaled white flowers which in autumn give way to very visible bunches of red berries also called chess apples, much sought after by birds. They are edible, but to be palatable they need to be kept until just going over.

Its leaves are remarkable for as they unfurl in early spring, they do so upright looking rather like magnolia flowers. Leaves are quite thick and finely-toothed. They have a shiny upper surface and a furry underside that gives the pale appearance. Bark is smooth and grey and wood is hard and like hornbeam has found use in stool legs and as cogs in wooden machinery. In ancient times, the Irish called it 'fionncholl' - white hazel.

Whitebeam is an hermaphrodite -both male and female parts are on the same flower - so self-propagation is easy. Having said that, this tree has something of a reputation for shall we say 'putting it about' with its relatives, giving rise to such raunchy variants as 'bastard service' (crossed with rowan), Arran, cliff and Wilmott's whitebeam amongst others. The clues with these various progeny are that the leaves are lobed to various different degrees. You will need to be a quite a sleuth to follow the trail of who was with whom in the whitebeam world, as for example Arran whitebeam (endangered and endemic to Arran) is a cross between cliff whitebeam and rowan.

So in fact it occurs to me that maybe it is rowan (mountain ash) who is the main suspect here. Yes, young man, you may well look at your shoes!

Wild service in a garden on Longridge. If you see one in the wild it's probably an indicator of ancient woodland. Leaves have distinctive pointed lobes at the base.

Flowers - Wiki Commons by BernH

132

Wild Service

(*Sorbus torminalis*)

This is a rare and fascinating tree. I've only ever seen two in the wild - it's a slow-growing native with some interesting stories - so I was delighted to hear of one in a garden on Longridge, backing onto the woods. This one is a relative youngster, about 6m high, which they planted 10 to 12 years ago and is clearly flourishing in its location.

Its very distinctive leaves have pointed lobes like maple, but with an extra pair of deeper triangular lobes near the base. In autumn these turn a coppery red, and in spring you'll see clusters of cream flowers of five petals each. In winter it can be identified by its lime green hairless buds. The flowers are hermaphrodite - both male and female elements are held within each flower.

Young trunk at left, and mature trunk above showing squares or chequers.

Historically the berries were made into an alcoholic drink and the trunk of the mature tree is fissured into small square shapes and this may be why it is also referred to as chequers.

Opinion is split over whether pubs known as The Chequers have been named after the alcoholic drink or the classic pub game. To add to these tangled theories is the reverse one that as the Latin for beer is cervisia, it was the drink that named the tree.

If you thought that was complicated, other tree species related to wild service (in the rose family Rosaceae), are rowan, whitebeam, mountain ash and excuse my French - 'bastard service' (a hybrid of rowan and whitebeam).

Although eagerly devoured by birds, the fruit is hard to digest and it seems that only the wood pigeon that has has a tough enough digestive system to soften the seeds, which also need a hot summer for germination.

This tree in the wild is often an indicator of ancient woodland mainly due to another style of propagation. It is able to reproduce by suckers, so often this means that the offspring are never far from the parent. Please let me know if you spot any of these in our local woods.

Ancient woodland is a special but threatened habitat and now accounts for only around 2.4% of the UK. It's defined as woodland that has existed since 1600 in England and Wales, and 1750 in Scotland - that's when reasonably reliable maps were first produced. It needs to have been largely un-touched by human development, and is likely to be home to a very diverse and rare range of flora and fauna. Some of the woodlands around Sheepscombe are defined as ancient, including Blackstable, Lord's and Lady's and Buckholt Wood by Cranham.   (DEFRA database)

Traditionally our Prime Ministers have Chequers in Buckinghamshire as their country residence. It seems they like to retreat there in times of trouble, but it is not recorded whether they resort to the eponymous alcohol or the board game to take their minds off current woes.

(This tree is on private land)

~~~~

Tree markings - what do they mean? The coloured marks on some trees in Lord's and Lady's Wood* are made in preparation for an autumn/winter's woodland management work. The pink generally indicates a tree to be removed, blue marks indicate retained trees and the path of trees to be pulled out to minimise disturbance elsewhere. Trees that can safely be left to decay in situ are preserved for the benefit of the wider woodland ecosystem.**

These woods are some of the finest examples of 'Continuous Cover Forestry' practised anywhere in the country. Our forestry consultant reviews the woodland compartments periodically and selects which trees to promote and which to remove. Each time we make an 'intervention' this manipulation of the canopy creates a competitive advantage for selected trees. It also allows increased light penetration down to the forest floor, thus improving growing conditions for the understorey trees, the shrub layer and lower ground flora.

(see pages *11 and **148)   Matt Stanway (NT)

Willow

Goat Willow (Salix caprea)
Crack Willow (Salix fragilis), White Willow (Salix alba)

Toad of Toad Hall, river banks, cricket, slender drooping branches, willow is an integral part of our country's identity. There are twelve species, and a bewildering number of hybrids (willow is very cross-compatible) including corkscrew, weeping, creeping, cricket bat, black, dwarf, bay willow and osier.

Most willows have a thick, gnarly bark on the main trunk, which soon branches and smoothes to become those "willowy" twigs that are so characteristic. Leaves in general are long and narrow, although notably on goat willow they are much more rounded, with crinkled edges and a downy underside. Leaves

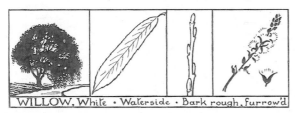

WILLOW. White · Waterside · Bark rough, furrow'd

of the white willow are whiter underneath, and in the wind give a silvery wave impression.

Willows tend to flower before they leaf in April/May and the yellow male catkins and female green catkins grow on different trees. This makes willow highly reliant on insects for pollination, but it does have another method of propagation - twigs and branches will grow if planted in the ground.

When a female catkin is pollinated it produces very fine, light, downy seeds. These have no endosperm (food supply) and thus have a short life, and need to land on moist ground so that they can germinate quickly.

Crack willow is so-called for a branch's tendency to snap under its own weight - it is less supple than other willows. The bark is deeply furrowed and the leaves are generally a darker green. Goat or pussy willow is easily identified by its more rounded leaves and those delightful silky round catkin buds.

Cricket bat willow (Salix alba Caerulea), is a native to the UK, where it is grown and selected specifically for our cricket bat industry. Straight, knot-free growth is essential and saplings are planted at a specific spacing to encourage tall straight growth as they compete for light. Each is carefully protected from livestock nibbling and any buds are regularly rubbed off to prevent side growth

Early spring **willow** in the Coldstream field, and its trunk. Goat willow catkins and weeping willow leaves.

and knots in the wood. You'll often see willow pollarded (cropped to above deer-nibbling height) and new growth is widely used in fence or basket-making.

I asked Susan Early about her willow business, having often spotted bundles of it stacked by their home on Far End Lane.

"There are around 400 species of willow, but not all work well for basket-making and sculptures. I buy the majority of my willow from growers on the Somerset levels. I buy 'bolts' of willow that have been sorted and graded, choosing different varieties for various projects I am making and also for teaching.

I only grow a very small amount of willow in Sheepscombe, a variety called Nancy Saunders which produces a very fine rod and I use this to make my smaller sculptures, fine baskets and wall decorations. Willow is dormant between November and February when they are harvested, the coppice stools from where the rods grow are cut close to the ground leaving a stump that will shoot as the sap rises again ready to be cut the following year.

I mainly use Salix triandra Black Maul, which is ideal for basket-making and is extremely pliable. This willow is often boiled creating a 'buff' golden brown finish, stripped producing a white rod and steamed creating a very dark brown colour. The different varieties of willow provide subtle colour variation. Dicky Meadows is a favourite of mine that has long fine elegant rods and a soft green colour, Brittany Green is a strong dark pliable rod, Flanders Red is very robust with a lovely red colour and particularly good for outside structures.

All the willows I use have different qualities for different plans, I mainly weave with willow with its 'bark on'. The willow will have been completely dried after cutting, stored and then it will be soaked for up to a week and left to mellow until it is pliable and ready to weave."

Susan's work can be found at: guildcrafts.org.uk/members/susan-early

It supports a wide range of moth and butterfly larvae, and is the primary food source of the Purple Emperor butterfly. Willow bark is still used in the preparation of leather as it is a source of tannin, and also produces salicin which was once used for pain relief and is a pre-cursor to aspirin.

So if life or politics is giving you a headache this summer, why not find yourself a grassy riverbank, lean back against a willow in the dappled light and chew on a piece of bark? I'm sure Ratty would approve.

(This tree is on private land - but it is visible from the road)

The **wych elm** on the right of the track, 100m into Workmans Woods from Far End. Distinctive large pointed serrated leaf often with 'horns' and asymmetric base.

Wych Elm

(Ulmus glabra)

I'd been looking for ages for this one, but I clearly wasn't tuned in properly, because now they're revealing themselves all over the place in this valley and elsewhere. There's quite a few hanging over the last bit of road before Far End.

With so much hazel around here, it's easy to miss wych, which can look similar. Key identifiers are large serrated leaves that are asymmetrical at the base, and a pointed tip often with two side 'horns'. English elm leaves have the

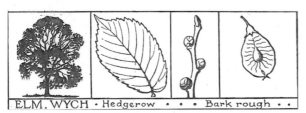

same characteristics as the wych but are smaller, more rounded, and lack the 'horns'.

The bark is grey brown, starting smooth but growing more fissured with age. For winter ID you'll find elm (of both types) generally have a more pitted bark than hazel and lack multiple stems.

Wych elm flowers are purple sprays at the far end of the twigs, and these appear early in the year before the leaves. In late spring you may spot the distinctive circular papery seeds on the ground, a surprise sprinkling amongst all the beech leaves. The seed sits in the middle of a small 'wing' called a samara.

But there's nothing witchy about this tree - the name probably refers to the pliable nature of its branches. Mediaeval Welsh archers used wych elm for their longbows while the English used yew.

Before the 1900s, elm dominated our forests and landscapes, and led Nicholas Culpeper - 17th century herbalist and botanist - to state that they were "one of the most commonest English trees, overlooking Nature's seasons". It even features in Constable's 1831 painting: 'Salisbury Cathedral From the Meadows'.

Branch and twig formation with samaras in spring.

Like alder, elm is resistant to water and rot and was once popular for boat and house-building and also for coffins and water-pipes, before cast iron came along.

Many birds are fond of the seeds, and the leaves provide food for moth caterpillars, including the peppered and white-spotted pinion. Caterpillars of the white-letter hairstreak butterfly feed almost exclusively on elm leaves and this species has declined dramatically since Dutch elm disease arrived in the UK.

In mythology (as in archery) both elm and yew are connected with death and the transition into the Underworld. Elm was once used to make coffins, where maybe its resilience in soil played a part in this choice. Known (like beech) to suddenly drop its boughs without warning, a chilling saying grew up: "Elm hateth man, and waiteth".

On a more positive note, an Italian tradition was to grow elm in vineyards to shade and protect the vines and to give the plant a structure to grow on. This 'marriage' of the elm and the vine was taken up by the Roman poet Ovid who in his Metamorphoses, recounts the myth of Vertumnus and Pomona. Vertumnus takes the shape of an old woman and urges the reluctant goddess Pomona to marriage by pointing to the vine in her orchard.

Elm beetle larvae feeding-tunnels in the trunk. (Wikipedia)

I'm there with elm actually, doing what I can to support vineyards.

Foxglove Tree *(Paulownia tomentosa)*
Willow Podocarp *(Podocarpus salignus)*
Japanese Maki *(Podocarpus macrophyllus)*
Mexican Weeping Pine *(Pinus patula)*

Nestling half way along Far End Lane under a fringe of more traditional ash, beech, oak and hazel, the sunny terraced garden at Knapp Cottage is chock full of exotic and delightful tree and plant species, all lovingly planted and tended since the current owners moved there in the 1980s. Theirs is a garden designed from scratch.

Possibly the most dramatic individual in residence, the **foxglove tree,** looks like it has been lifted straight out of the jungle, and when I visited I was half expecting David Bellamy (the naturalist) to pop out from behind one of its gigantic leaves.

This fast-growing deciduous tree was introduced in the 1800s from China where its wood was used for furniture making. If left to its own devices, it produces fragrant pinkish-purple flowers very similar to its more familiar namesake. When coppiced back to old wood as it is here, it will produce huge, soft heart-shaped leaves - up to 60cm across - on very long stems, but this method prevents maturity and flowering. I'm told that the leaves are so heavy that when they fall in autumn there's an audible thud!

The foxglove tree needs to be planted in a sheltered spot away from direct sunlight and strong winds, both of which can damage the leaves, and due to its rapid growth should be well watered and in a rich soil. This specimen is around 15-20 years old and about 5m tall.

Willow podocarp is an attractive, graceful tree that originates from Chile and surprisingly is a conifer, not a willow. Standing around 5m tall against a sheltered border it produces masses of willow-like needles on arching and drooping branches. Old foliage is dark green which gives a lovely contrast to the light green of spring growth.

Podocarp is a hardy evergreen and distantly related to the yew - the resemblance can be seen in the trunk which is reddish-brown, rather fibrous and peels off in strips - and the small red berries that appear on older trees.

Foxglove tree (above)
and **willow podocarp** (below)

Japanese maki (left) and
Mexican weeping pine (right)
at Knapp Cottage

Cut wood has a yellowish hue, and is straight grained. It is highly moisture resistant and therefore useful for furniture and construction at least where it's plentiful at home in Chile. This one is over 20 years old. Willow podocarp enjoys light shade away from strong winds in moist but well-drained soil and is reasonably frost hardy.

Their **Japanese maki** is another evergreen conifer that doesn't look like one. Also known as the 'yew plum' pine or 'Buddhist' pine, its branches are feathery and covered with shorter, narrow lance-like leaves. Plants are either male or female (dioecious) and if pollinated the female will display attractive clusters of blue and purple fruits near branch tips - this one is probably a female.

Maki is a hardy individual and like willow podocarp is related to the yew, visible through its berries and bark, and is happiest in a shady spot with rich well-drained soil tending to neutral or acidic. The tree is normally really slow growing, and after the 15-20 years this one has spent in this garden, this one is tall for its age at around 3.5m high. In Hong Kong, maki is prized as a Feng Shui tree, for its pleasing shape and the fact that it can be grown in a container and trained as a bonsai.

Standing tall near the back of the garden, the **Mexican weeping pine** is a graceful sight with feathery soft needles on long spreading branches that hang down like curtains. This one is only about 12 years old but has clearly shot up, now reaching 5 to 6 m!

Patula means 'spreading' and it is a native of the highlands of Mexico, so is tolerant of our cooler climate. It is popular in the UK as an ornamental tree in parks and gardens. The trunk - like many pines - is rough, craggy, and reddish-brown. It is happy in full sun, in a sheltered spot otherwise cold winds can turn the needles brown. Weeping pine prefers neutral or slightly acid well-draining soil. Cones are about 10cm long with shiny scales.

It's widely cultivated around the world, usefully fast-growing, and in Kenya accounts for around a third of all plantations. This is not surprising given that the wood is used in particle board manufacture, makes good firewood and when tapped, yields a resin used in the production of turpentine and paint.

The owner told me her secret for gardening success was simple: hard work and lots of local donkey poo!

(These trees are on private land)

Ivy *(Hedera helix)*
Clematis *(Clematis vitalba)*
Mistletoe *(Viscum album)*

If there were a Cluedo® of the plant world, I would imagine that Ivy, Clematis and Mistletoe would have a lot of explaining to do. Much of our mistletoe is on our whitebeams, and the other suspects are everywhere to be seen in our hedgerows and woodlands, climbing or living on our trees.

Ivy often gets a bad press. It's commonly associated with decaying trees, neglected buildings and no doubt also framing the doorway of many a woodland goblin. But in fact today's reality and yesterday's folk-law teach us just the opposite. Yes, it will climb rapidly on any vertical structure if left unattended and clings on tight with specialist hairs strong enough to pull out mortar. But actually ivy is not parasitic, doesn't damage trees at all as it has its own root-system for obtaining nutrients and water. This variant, 'helix' is the climbing one, while ground-cover ivy is 'hibernica'.

In folk-law and classical cultures Ivy seems to have been a big player - The Roman god Bacchus (never without a drink in his hand), was often depicted wearing a wreath of ivy and grapevines, the former supposedly to ward off drunkenness. Also favoured as symbol of fidelity, priests might present a wreath of ivy to newly married couples.

In winter the black berries growing in clusters provide welcome sustenance for blackbirds, wood pigeons and thrushes who seek them out for their high fat content. Ivy flowers late, and in autumn wasps, bees and hover-flies feast on the nectar and pollen as they prepare for hibernation. Ivy's evergreen leaves are dark and glossy with visible pale veins. Those of juvenile plants have 3-5 lobes and a pale underside. When mature the leaves are oval or heart shaped without lobes.

Clematis has an altogether better reputation as evidenced by its nicknames 'traveller's joy' and 'old man's beard'. It is a vigorous woody climbing vine and scrambles haphazardly through our hedgerows and the edge of our woodlands. In autumn and early winter it is easy to spot the hairy seed-heads called achenes, especially with the low sun behind them.

Clematis leaves are pinnate compound with 5-7 tooth-edged leaflets arranged

- On Trees of Sheepscombe -

Ivy, clematis and **mistletoe**
spotted locally. So whodunnit?

either side along a stem. In summer the white flowers of this common variety appear in clusters with visible stamens.

Before we sing clematis' praises too highly it's worth noting that it was once thought to be doing the Devil's work by wrapping round and strangling any plant it could find - and to this day many gardeners consider it to be an invasive weed. In the past it seems to have been more useful though, lending its stems to rope, basket-making and for twine to bind sheaves of corn.

Mistletoe. Surely the villain of the piece? Parasitic, fleshy and poisonous in every part, mistletoe is at once other-worldly, yet has become an integral part of our Christmas ritual. Most often found in apple, lime, poplar and whitebeam trees, the growths form a green globe which can reach a meter across and easy to spot in the otherwise bare host tree.

The translucent berries are not especially attractive to most birds, but are irresistible to the mistle-thrush and blackcap. When wiped off the beak, or passed through the digestive system the gluey gel surrounding the seed helps it to stick on the branch. As the new plant grows, its roots invade the tree and the deed is done. Mistletoe comes in a male or female variety - dioecious - and like holly it is the female plant which bears the berry.

It is clear that this plant has a deep and rich seam of symbolism. Roman Historian Pliny the Elder wrote of the Celts: *"Here we must mention the reverence felt for this plant by the Gauls. The Druids—for thusly are their priests named—hold nothing more sacred than the mistletoe and the tree that bears it, as long as that tree be an oak... Mistletoe is very rarely encountered; but when they do find some, they gather it, in a solemn ritual..."*

And the whole kissing thing? There are plenty of legends, but I like this one:

When the Norse goddess Frigga gave birth to her son Baldur, she wanted to protect him more than anything else in the world. So she made each and every plant, animal, and inanimate object promise never to harm him. Unfortunately Frigga overlooked the mistletoe plant, and the mischievous god Loki took advantage of this. He tricked another god into killing Baldur with a spear made from mistletoe. It is said that mistletoe berries represent Frigga's tears and that it was decided ever after, that couples should kiss under mistletoe so as to bring love rather than death.

So, in the cold light of day, was it Mistletoe in the hall, Ivy by the balustrade or that devilish Clematis in the kitchen garden?

Standing dead-wood provides a ready dry habitat for birds, bats and insects. The wood softens with age and is easy to hollow out or bore into. Watch out for woodpeckers!

Fallen branches or trunks in contact with the ground, are much wetter and provide a good habitat for worms, woodlice, millipedes, ferns, fungi and mosses.

In Lord's and Lady's Woods beech is the predominant species of fallen and standing timber,though there is ash, oak and conifer too.

Standing
and fallen dead-wood
(Psittacus mortuus)

We humans are pretty coy about what happens to us after we die and go to *join the choir invisible.* We have all sorts of rituals and euphemisms to help us make sense of the unknown and to draw a veil across the inevitable. Thank goodness we can rely on religion (or Python) to help us through.* Trees, on the other hand have no such assistance, and are destined to play out their life and death pretty much in the same place, and in clear view. But thanks to this very public display we can learn a lot about the ecosystems in our woodlands, especially at a time when we are more aware than ever of their importance.

Covering the tree from its earliest sapling moments, the bark (like our own skin) is there to protect it from harm; infections, insects and fungi as well as to conserve water. Whether by damage, old age, lightning, storm or the work of man, once a tree is toppled or its bark is severely compromised, the agents of decay begin their work.

It is a fascinating and complex process. Many other organisms rely on the goodness they can glean

Bark beetle tracks revealed on a wind-blown oak - the ivy is still alive.

and the shelter afforded by the wood. Finally all remaining nutrients are recycled as they dissolve back into the soil along with nitrogen. The carbon stored by the tree in its lifetime is locked back into the soil rather than being released to the atmosphere. Fallen logs can also add to soil stability, especially on sloping ground.

Dead and dying wood will find itself colonised by a host of organisms and creatures. The sapwood (new wood) and cambium (growing cells) will be invaded by wood-boring bark-beetles, fungi, lesser stag beetles and longhorns. Predators will follow such as spiders, wasps and in the Scots pine the robber fly which feeds on longhorn beetle larvae.

Mites, millipedes, hover-flies and woodlice are associated with the mid-stage of decay - these 'saproxylic' invertebrates are dependent on dead or decaying wood (or on organisms that are themselves dependent on dead wood). Fungi set to work decaying the less nutritious heartwood, and as their thread-like mycelia penetrate the layers they allow passage for other organisms working in the latter stages of decay. Finally the wood turns to humus, and the cycle is complete.

King Alfred's Cakes fungus, once used to carry a spark from fire to fire.

Standing dead-wood trunks, 'snags', provide a very different habitat to fallen trunks or branches. Snags remain drier, and woodland birds such as woodpeckers and crested tits will hollow out roosting sites from the soft rotting wood, while owls and bats will make a home of any natural hollow. Raptors find tall snags ideal as a lookout while hunting - there are clear views all round. Woodpeckers come to standing deadwood for a rich supply of bugs and beetles just below the surface. Their hollow knocking is a classic sound around the valley.

Fallen or 'wind-blown' trunks, along with fallen or deliberately piled branches are in contact with the damp forest floor and as a result, decay will be faster and soggier. A different cohort of organisms will colonise here. And as any woodland child will tell you, under most logs can be found worms, woodlice, centipedes, slugs and ants in abundance. Fungi, mosses and ferns will also thrive, being moisture lovers. The gaps between logs make ideal shelter and passage-ways for voles, mice and other small vertebrates who wish to scurry about their daily business while remaining out of sight of the raptors up in the snags or the fox on his rounds.

Threats to this important habitat can be as simple as too much tidiness in parks and woodland gardens, and indeed our own gardens.

So if questioned as to why you have a pile of dead-wood in your garden you can answer *"it's not dead, it's resting!"*

*It's Monty Python Week in this house.

Winter tree identification

You are initially looking for bud or twig symmetry about the branch, and it's best if you're under the tree looking up at the branches against the sky.

For trees with **opposing** buds or twigs a useful acronym is: **MADCAPS Horse.**

Maples - Sycamore, Norway and field maple - you may see black-spotted old sycamore leaves on the ground, and field maple has bark rather like a 'flake' chocolate.

Ash - branches that swoop up at the end with a single black bud.

Dogwood - small to medium sized and new growth is dark red or orange.

CAPrifloacae - Elder, guelder rose, snowberry. Small to medium-sized.

Horse chestnut - branches curve up at the end with a single sticky bud.

And **Spindle** - small to medium-sized with straight stems and pink berries.

If the buds or twigs are **alternate**, then your main options locally are:

Beech - smooth bark, branches and twigs seem to fan out in layers.

Oak - rough trunks, major branches, and three small buds at the twig tips.

Hazel - multi-stemmed and often with catkins.

Wych elm - a more pitted bark than hazel and generally lacks multiple stems. Twiglets seem to grow at 90 degrees to the stem like a tiny ladder.

Lime - look for suckers growing from the base, buds zig-zag on the twigs.

Silver birch - silvery fractured bark and slender branch/twig appearance.

Alder (horizontal branching, catkins and cones on the branch, near water)

Willow - v rough bark, slender branching, buds tight to the twig, near water.

Hawthorn or Blackthorn - both are spiky and untidy, hawthorns may have a few old red berries remaining, blackthorn buds grow along the spines.

Trees of Sheepscombe Quiz 1

Test yourself on some of the trees in this book!

1 - Dinosaurs may have munched on this once.

2 - This has a flaky bark which helps shed pollution.

3 - Often coppiced and used for walking sticks or fence posts.

4 - A very hard wood, and once used for making Shillelaghs.

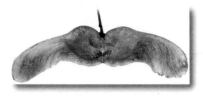

5 - Whose winged seeds are nearly at 180 degrees to each other?

6 - On which tree might you have once found "The King's mark"? (no photo)

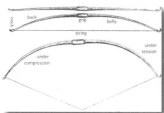

7 - Longbows were made from this tree.

8 - Don't picnic under this one, especially on a windy day!

9 - Loves water, and "bleeds" red when cut.

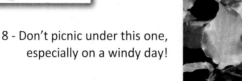

10 - Huge leaves and named after a flower.

11 - The bark of this one often has a marked spiral pattern.

12 - This tree's leaves tremble tremendously, (no photo).

Answers on page 156

Trees of Sheepscombe
Quiz 2

Wiki

Answers on page 156

154

Reflection

I must have been about twelve or fourteen years old, and I was cycling through our local woods. It was a route I often took, from our house, the mile or so to friends who lived on the other side. The woods and commons were our playground, our escape, our nature and our nurture. Complete freedom. Sun, rain or wind. Day or night. And night-time in a windy wood - that was edgy!

This particular occasion it was just past dusk. Rather a risky time to be cycling there perhaps, but I knew every turn in the path, every tree and root and lumpy bit of ground. No lights, or if I was lucky the dim glow of a nearly spent Ever-Ready cycle lamp, if it hadn't leapt off its bracket and into the bracken. Actually I could see more without it, especially if the moon was up.

That evening there was still a bit of a glow in the sky, probably that purple-going-into-dark-blue just as the stars come out. On the edge of the Common I paused and looked up at some of the trees against the sky. It was late autumn and windy.

With unusual clarity I was struck by the presence of some of the trees, the characters there. The shapes and the sounds that they threw down. Some stark and angular, creaking and groaning in the wind. Others softer and more graceful. Still noisy but less threatening. I began to try to work out if some were happy or troubled, healthy or diseased.

But it was time to go. It was now almost fully dark and the orange street lights of my friends' road were still half a mile away, round the pond, over the bridge and along the edge of the golf course.

Since then, whenever I have had the choice of where to live, there have had to be woodlands. Unable to resist this environment I trained in Bushcraft in 2014 and as a Forest School Leader in 2016 and my connection with the natural world deepened.

Woodlands are the antithesis and balance to our screen-driven frenetic lifestyle. Time is a slow mistress under the canopy. Cycles of slumber, growth, full glory and release take a year to play out. To properly get alongside them I find I need to go at their pace, to spend an hour or more just wandering, gazing, sitting and being.

Acknowledgements

Many Sheepscombe villagers kindly opened their gardens to me to photograph their special tree and often tell me its story. I'm grateful to all the authors and sources whose books and pages I have leafed and scrolled through for nuggets of information - I've learnt so much along the way. Under the banner of Sheepscombe News from 2018-22, I was lucky enough to find an outlet for my monthly writings. So thank you Jackie and Rob Jones who were my Editor and Proof-reader respectively (any errors that you find are mine alone). Thank you to all the humans in my photographs - especially to Julie and to Alessio. I'm also grateful to Julie for her Herbal Medicine advice, the map and because she listens to trees with me. Thanks Tom Griffin and Matt Stanway of the National Trust and Kate Gamez of Natural England who have shared their knowledge of the woods. There's an excellent local booklet on Workman's Wood (see bibliography). Thanks to my parents for choosing to bring us up near to Ruislip Woods, and to my dear friends the English family and Moomyn the dog for endless adventures there. And before I go full Oscar - thank you to the trees - you know who you are.

The Spirit of the Woods. This carving near the Ebworth Centre was inspired by Laurie Lee who referred to John Workman as the 'Spirit of the Woods'. It was commissioned by John from Westonbirt Arboretum.

Trees Quiz 1 answers. 1: Gingko 2: London Plane 3: Hazel 4: Blackthorn 5: Field Maple 6: Oak 7: Yew 8: Beech 9: Alder 10: Foxglove Tree 11: Sweet Chestnut 12: Aspen

Trees Quiz 2 answers. 1: Cedar of Lebanon 2: Wild Pear 3: Fern or cut-leaf Beech 4: Eucalyptus 5: Black Mulberry 6: Juniper 7: Tulip Tree 8: Walnut 9: Whitebeam

Bibliography

Books and websites referred to in general:

Collins Complete Guide to British Trees - Paul Sterry - Collins (2007)

Britain's Trees - Jo Woolf - National Trust (2020)

Tree Wisdom - Jacqueline Memory Paterson - Thorsons (1996)

The Woodland Way - Ben Law - Permanent Publications (2008)

Norwegian Wood - Lars Mytting - Quercus Publishing (2015)

The Man Who Made Things out of Trees - Robert Penn - Penguin (2016)

Look and Find Out 'Trees' - W Percival Westell and Kate Harvey, illustrations [including the tree-tables used in this book] by Doris Meyer - Macmillan (1938)

Woodland Management (A Practical Guide - Chris Starr - Crowood (2013)

Workmans Wood - Tarran, Knight, Skinner and Workman - Sheepscombe History Society (2002).   ~~   WoodlandTrust.org.uk Sheepscombe.org

nationaltrust.org.uk Gov.uk//Natural-England   RHS.org.uk Wikipedia.org

Woodlands.co.uk TreeSpiritWisdom.com WildLifeTrusts.org PlantLore.com

BBC.co.uk/Nature and Plants ForestryEngland.uk HollandAndBarrett.com

GloucesterWildlifeTrust.co.uk EatWeeds.co.uk TreesForLife.org.uk

Wood-Database.com GoodWoodsTimber.co.uk ForestSchoolAssociation.org

Subject-specific resources:

Alder	TreesPlantsFlowers.Blogspot.co.uk David Hopkins pers comms Monumentaltrees.com
Ash	Ancient-Wisdom.com/treelore
Aspen	As general list
Beech & Cultivars	Barcham.co.uk 4SeasonsTreeCare.co.uk Keele.ac.uk FedcoSeeds.com
John Workman Tree	Tom Griffin (National Trust) pers comms
Silver Birch & Blackthorn	As general list
Catalpa	Nash-News.com
Cedar of Lebanon	Arboriculture.Wordpress.com MonumentalTrees.com DownToEarthHomesteaders.com

Cherry	BurlyBeaver.com TheSpruceCrafts.com WoodMagasine.com MedicalNewsToday.com
Dawn Redwood	R Paterson and E Skinner - pers comms Cotf.edu/Mesozoic Deepdale-Trees.co.uk Conifers.org ChewValleyTrees.co.uk
Dead wood	Acompletetreecare.com BugLife.org.uk Blogs.tcv.org.uk//TheDeadGoodDeadwoodBlog ConservationEvidence.com
Elder	BelvoirFruitFarms.co.uk WildHealingGarden.co.uk
Elm	As general list
Eucalyptus	TheJoyOfPlants.co.uk Agriculture.gov.au indigenousBoats.Blogspot.com Collections.MuseumsVictoria.com.au
False Acacia	LiveScience.com SelectTree.CalPoly.edu Herbal-Supplement-Resource.com Nature.com
Field Maple	TheViolinSite.com NaturalMedicinalHerbs.net
Gingko	LiveScience.com SelectTree.CalPoly.edu Herbal-Supplement-Resource.com Nature.com ClassicalChineseMedicine.org
Guelder Rose	Indigo-Herbs.co.uk TreeGrowing.tcv.org.uk Thyra2005.Blogspot.com
Hawthorn	As general list
Hazel & Holly	As general list
Hornbeam	Wayside and Woodland trees - E Step - F Warne (1904)
Horse Chestnut	Sloely.Com GardeningKnowHow.com
Ivy, Clem. & Mistle.	FrustratedGardener.com TheSpruce.com MistletoeFoundation.co.uk Bernheim.org Alvin-Portal.org NatureWalk.yale.edu
Juniper	PlantLife.org.uk DunnetBayDistillers.co.uk Medical Herbalism - Hoffmann - Inner Traditions (2003) Kate Gamez (Natural England) pers comms
Knapp Cottage	Architectural Plants - Christine Shaw - Collins ArchitecturalPlants.com BBC.co.uk Barcham.co.uk
Larch	HighlandTitles.com - S Borland ScotlandForestry.gov.uk
Lilac	LearnReligions.com ParamountPlants.com DavesGarden.com TheWhittlingGuide.com
Lime	NaturalLore.Wordpress.com CountryLife.co.uk

London Plane	EnglishWoodlandsTimber.co.uk Londonist.com
Monkey Puzzle	EdenProject.com RawEdiblePlants.Blogspot.com
Mulberry	TheClassroom.com MentalFloss.com MorusLondinium.org GreenAndVibrant.com BiddleSawyersSilks.com
Oak	TheNewForestGuide.co.uk
Pear	SavilleFurniture.com RowdenAtelier.com Wise-Geek.com MythEncyclopedia.com
Poplar	CelticCreations.Wordpress.com ScienceHistory.org
Scots Pine	TotalPoles.co.uk TreeBlog.co.uk
Spindle	ButterfyConservation.org LegendaryDartmoor.co.uk NorfolkWildlifeTrust.org.uk
Sweet Chestnut	Blog.Italian-Pewter.co.uk (recipe)
Sycamore	Tolpuddlemartyrs.org.uk
Tulip Tree	SurvivalSherpa.Wordpress.com Deepdale-Trees.co.uk Henriettes-Herb.com
Walnut	WildHealingGarden.co.uk ~ Julie Wood Lapada.org CastleHoward.co.uk ~ Maria Ellis TheSpruceCrafts.com
Wayfaring Tree	As general list
Whitebeam & Rowan	BugWomanLondon.com
Wild Service	HeartOfEnglandForest.com BugWomanLondon.com Distribn. of the Wild Service Tree - P Roper (1993) DEFRA database.
Willow	Susan Early pers comms CricketBatWillow.com Guildcrafts.org.uk/members/Susan-Early
The Woods	Workmans Wood - Sheepscombe History Society UKSouthWest.net CotswoldsAONB.org.uk Gov.uk - Cotswold Commons and Beechwoods Tom Griffin and Matt Stanway (National Trust) and Elisabeth Skinner pers comms
Wych Elm	Sussex-Butterflies.org.uk
Yew	MedievalChronicals.com

Published by
WhiteSpringBooks.co.uk

First edition
February 2023
© Peter Collings-Wells
All Rights Reserved.

Design, layout and all photography by PCW unless credited otherwise.

Printed by Wheatley Printers of Stroud, using 100% recycled paper from certified sustainable sources.

Please note: The contents of this book are provided for information only. Always consult a Medical Herbalist or your Doctor, before using or eating plants or tree products, especially if you are breastfeeding, pregnant, or on any medication or have any physical or mental disorder or allergy.

50p from the sale of each book is donated to the Woodland Trust.

This page: The beech tunnel down from the Birdlip road. Opposite: Looking across to Beech Wood from the Far End post box and the author in his element in 2014.